To the wonder: Patricia

Living with Wonder

Living with Wonder

Leland Wilson

WORD BOOKS, PUBLISHER

Waco, Texas

LIVING WITH WONDER

Copyright © 1976 by Word, Incorporated, Waco, Texas.

All rights reserved.

Scripture quotations in this book are from the Revised Standard Version of the Bible, copyrighted 1946, 1952, © 1971, 1973 by the Division of Christian Education of the National Council of the Churches of Christ in the U.S.A., and are used by permission.

Printed in the United States of America

Library of Congress Catalog Card Number: 76-19543

ISBN: 0-87680-839-9

Contents

Places   *11*

People   *25*

Definings   *47*

Interpretings   *55*

Scatterings   *73*

Events   *89*

Trends   *101*

Images   *111*

Recorded here are ideas or impressions that have lingered with me. Like spring, they came forth after the planting of experience, the germination of reflection, and the growth of placing them on paper.

These are impressions of people I have known, of places I have been, of events that have impinged upon my life. Here also are understandings that have unfolded in metaphor.

Perhaps there will be value in sharing them since they give both *personal* and *religious* meanings. In the personal meanings of others, we can often identify our own meanings that were previously vague and indistinct. I hope a reader will find such identity, or that which comes by its countermeasure, reaction. In religious meanings, concerning as they do the transcendent in life, the mystery of a presence, we must be in constant search-and-share missions —the two processes are comingled. While impressions are shared, that is part of the search of the sharer. Impressions are the raw material for living with wonder.

LELAND WILSON

⸙⟦Places⟧⸙

Aline is on the plains of western Oklahoma. Five miles from that little town I spent all but the first three years of my childhood and youth.

Now I find deep pleasure in riding down the sandy road that bordered our farm. Riding—the horse has so many more possibilities than the automobile! There is the grace and vigor of the run, and there is the slow, rhythmic walk that lets the reins fall slack. The horse continues with his own head, and there is time for yours to think. There is time to reflect. There is time to commune, spirit with Spirit, not shattered for the moment by the movement of machines or the voice of another human being.

It is a road that some days sees only the mailman. It is a road that opens a broad sunset, bright and beautiful. It is lined on both sides with barbed-wire fence to remind cattle that their freedom has bounds and that if they try to go through or beyond those bounds it will hurt. Caught in the fences are tumbleweeds. They have been snapped from their roots, and the wind sends them flying, tumbling over and over, until finally they are caught and held by the fence. Between the road and the fence is a blaze of wild sunflowers. They are rough, coarse weeds; yet they bear flowers that border on beauty and defy sand and sun. Sometimes the beauty of life is found in the wild and the rough, the uncultivated—that which faces the harshness of the world and still blooms.

Here and there is a windmill, the most fascinating of all machinery. Striking are its parts and angles and movements, yet simple its functioning as it pumps water into a large tank. It is one of the few machines powered from unrefined elements of creation. The wind blows, and the windmill does its work; no pollution rises from its turning. Yet in so simple a machine is a premonition of what is to come with machines, and that is what drives some idealistic Don Quixote out to battle a windmill. It is the premonition aroused by the windmill that makes it fascinating.

And there are fields of wheat. As farmers of this area— with their dark, leathery faces and their light foreheads, shielded by straw hats—move into those fields with combines, they understand the Scripture which says, "The harvest is plentiful, but the laborers are few; pray therefore the Lord of the harvest to send out laborers into his harvest" (Matt. 9:37–38). They know that Jesus was using the figure of grain to speak of people. But they know too that in these times, in this place, the grain is plentiful and the people are becoming few. In the small country church a mile away, they wonder if the future holds a harvest of people.

To ride along that road is to have time for memories. Over there is where the bootlegger lived and farmed during the days when the state was dry. Everyone knew he bootlegged whiskey—everyone but the county sheriff. A few years after I left there, even the sheriff learned about it and finally took him to jail. I remember working with that man in one of his fields. I was thirteen or fourteen, and we were taking bundles of barley and putting them into shocks. He became one of the first to shatter for me some myths of American life. In the little one-room white-frame schoolhouse—eight grades, twenty-five to thirty students— I had been taught that America was a democracy and that meant anybody could become president. Abraham Lincoln was offered as proof. The bootlegger was something of a cynic about government, and as I repeated to him what I had learned, he laughed at me and at the idea that there was equal opportunity and that everyone had a chance to be president. "Fat chance you have of being president," he said. His amusement wounded me at the time, but I think it was an introduction to reality.

The pleasure that comes in riding down that road is mixed with pain. My own memory and the memories of others are too acutely aware of those times I was foolish. The Apostle Paul set an example when he testified, "One thing I do, forgetting what lies behind and straining forward to what lies ahead, I press on toward the goal for the prize of the upward call of God in Christ Jesus" (Phil. 3:13–14). A good testimony, but difficult to duplicate.

It is good to go back down that same road, but I really cannot do it because it is not the same road. The place is not the same. The trees are different; the lay of the land is different. The landmarks have changed. The old farmhouse has been empty for several years. Unknown people came and broke its windows and took what they could find. The barn is slowly giving way to the elements. It is a question

15

how long the buildings will stand, but it is a question that no one bothers to pose. When the buildings finally crumble in the dirt and weeds, only the eyes of God will see.

It is not the same. I cannot go back.

My entrance into Washington, D.C., was in a military airplane. At nineteen, I first glimpsed the nation's capital. My early years had been spent in something other than a metropolis, but I saw photos—the Capitol, the White House, and monuments to Washington, Lincoln, and Jefferson. There was an aura of excitement about going to Washington.

The part of the plane in which I was riding had no windows. Through a tube, word was spoken that we were landing at Bolling Field. All the dreams of seeing Washington fed into the moment that I stepped out of the plane after we had landed. There, right ahead of me, was the Capitol dome, lighted and majestic in its whiteness. There was something awesome about seeing that building for the first time, and at night.

It was a rich moment, not destroyed by later, more sobering views of the city.

The year was 1964 and the place was eastern Nebraska. The thing was a bridge. I discovered it as I traveled to Lincoln by car, from the east, and missed a turn onto

Highway 6 going west from Des Moines. This was prior to the completion of the interstate system. I drove several miles south of Des Moines and finished crossing Iowa to the west on Highway 34. As I entered the state of "the Great Commoner," I met it—a colorful, rickety old bridge that raised questions of safety, as do all old bridges.

Obviously, speed had to be reduced and the crossing made cautiously. At the end of the clanking planks was an abrupt left turn. There, squarely in the middle of the highway, was what appeared to be a large privy—euphemistically called, in these days of sanitation, a comfort station. It did seem a strange location, but my puzzlement soon shifted when on closer examination it turned out to be a toll house! Two men were operating there, and while they were adequately attired, they had no uniforms. The shifty eyes of one made me wonder if two Nebraska bootleggers had just moved that little shack to the middle of the road without the knowledge of the highway department.

Then I saw a sign which read something like, "Free access, pay as you leave." Imagine that! But what good does free access do you?

When I stopped at the little shack, a booming voice demanded seventy cents from me for having crossed that rickety old bridge. Then I saw on the side of the little shack a crudely painted sign listing the charges. Cars with a driver, fifty cents; each additional passenger, ten cents. Pedestrians were only five cents. Had I known, my two passengers could have walked across and saved us some money.

My first reaction was anger and outrage at the immorality of charging to cross that rickety old bridge. Later I

17

weakened into amusement at thinking that two Nebraska bootleggers, the whole state, or someone was really working an "angle."

Ocean Grove, New Jersey, is a city set apart. It did not begin that way; there has been no papal recognition of immaculate conception. Along some childhood stream she floated,

> The dream-child moving through a land
>   Of wonders wild and new
> In friendly chat with bird or beast—
>   And half believe it true.
>
> And ever, as the story drained
>   The wells of fancy dry,
> And faintly strove that weary one
>   To put the subject by,
> "The rest next time—" "It *is* next time!"
>   LEWIS CARROLL
>   in *Alice's Adventures in Wonderland*

She crossed the threshold of a looking-glass house where everything was reversed. What had been an ordinary city became in illusion the Holy City, the New Jerusalem. By virtue, Ocean Grove would avoid what Jacques Ellul calls "thunder over the city," its curse and condemnation.

Proper dress, discreet disrobing to modest swim coverage at designated bathhouses only, will shade the skin and keep this place from becoming the fleshpot that marks other beaches. Serenity is not to be interrupted by the laughter of robust men and women; the ribald must not only be foreign, it should be unknown. Serenity is not to be broken by children playing ball in the park; suppose it should lead them to living like Babe Ruth or Joe Namath? "Remember the sabbath day, to keep it holy" (Exod. 20:8). Unlikely as it seems, Ocean Grove took form after the new covenant: "Remember the Lord's Day to keep it holy." What could be more profane than an automobile, that which drains our wealth, defiles the air we breathe, desecrates the landscape, determines our life station, and to which we give obeisance as an idol. The Lord's Day in Ocean Grove knows no such abomination. Not only is there no auto movement, the eyes of the holy city are shielded from the ugliness of Volkswagens, Pintos, Plymouths, and the most odious contraptions of all, the campers. Behind garage doors or dumped on the doorsteps of other cities go the junk heaps so that Ocean Grove may be spiritual.

The musty rooms, the cold damp weather even in June provoke complaints from the irreligious, but Ocean Grove is unmoved. She is a matriarch, like one from the old country whose mind has ceased to function, yet she continues to impose her will and dated ways upon everyone around. You can plead with her, cajole, threaten, but impassively she disconnects her hearing aid. She cares not for her family, nor for the rest of the world; she wants quiet and a Sunday of gathering herself in glorious procession down the middle of the streets to the great auditorium for another sermon by the sea.

Next door to Ocean Grove lives an adolescent, Asbury Park. He is a constant carnival. His boardwalk is bordered by expensive cheap rides and hucksters of trinkets. His raucous bleating is heard all the way to the Great City, and down the coast they come, searching for fun. They look for a laugh, some diversion.

19

Nothing satisfying here. The adolescent takes their money, and they leave, tired, disappointed. Asbury Park is like dime-store jewelry that comes in a sparkling package. It is like old movie sets that are mere façades, like the puffy cereals that contain primarily air. The city lacks authenticity, depth, and nourishment.

An adolescent beside a matriarch. But he is no "Graduate," and she is no "Mrs. Robinson." Oh, he does have the aimlessness of the Graduate but not the sexual curiosity. She has already realized that vision of the Apostle Paul's where there is "neither male nor female."

There is no generational love affair between these two. They do not even know the other exists. A Berlin Wall is built between them. To go from one to the other is not simply a geographic exercise, it is also an ideological experience.

We can thank God that in his creation and man's creation there is more than Ocean Grove and Asbury Park. If that were all, and even the thought is tragic, where would I choose to live? I think my choice would be Asbury Park. Why? Has it something to do with freedom? Is it the promise of adolescence, however pimpled, as contrasted with senility? Is it more honest than the pretension of the religious? Could it be a base craving for the carnival? Whatever, at least, it is alive, and it is preferable to death on the other side of the wall.

Disneyland is a fabulous, fairy-tale land where one delights in such exhibits and rides as the Haunted House, the Pirates of the Caribbean, and the Submarine Ride and marvels at the engineering and imagination that have gone into these devices.

After my second or third visit to Disneyland, I experienced a curious change in feeling. I found much less fascination with the mechanical. I had seen it. I knew what would happen. That was that. My interest turned to the people exhibits: the fairy-tale characters roaming around, the Pepsi Show with its touch of vaudeville, the stage productions. I could feel the dynamic of people speaking but not sure what they would say, of people laughing and sweating and stumbling and working. When the mechanical is with me too long, I enjoy all the more the aliveness and the unpredictability of the human.

Silver City, why do you draw me? What makes you a lure? What do you offer that not only attracts but satisfies, so that drinking I no longer thirst?

Perhaps it is the height—6,935 feet. Yet not height alone, for "the friendly skies of United" offer height but no solace. The Sierra Nevadas evoke a wonder that one cannot describe. My mind plays around the words of the psalmist—who can capture the depth and height of life as he? They say that Mr. Disney wanted to come here and sit upon the throne of Mineral King. But this is no Mickey Mouse place, and if it becomes another Magic Kingdom, surely that will be the end of the kingdom I find here.

Perhaps it's the remoteness—twenty-three miles from the highway. The journey in and up is slow and climbing, around sharp turns, some roadways surfaced, some dirt. It is preparation. The slow approach is in keeping with the time it requires to absorb the place. Remote but not solitary, it is open only in the summer, and there are those who come back year after year. For a few, it is a summer residence, sweet relief from the San Bernardino Freeway and endless meetings.

Perhaps it's the sequoias. Straight and tall they stand, unentangled by Watergates and Vietnams. Through the trees, the bluest of skies and the brightest patches of sun. Does it resurrect Eden? Yet the trees are not without evidence of their own tragedy. Lower limbs hang out stunted and dangling with death. Amid all the abundance, they could not get their share; they fall away early. Here and there, giant trees have fallen. No one noticed why or when. They are simply down. Though they occasionally give heat to our fire, mostly they are an encumbrance on our pathway. When the giants go down, unless we are directly in the pathway, they seem to affect our lives but little.

Perhaps it's the quiet, but it's never a still quiet. Even in the past-midnight moon, there is the continual murmur of waters falling across the rocks and plunging down the mountain. How can they keep coming? Is there no end? Your mystery draws me daily to sit beside you where your murmur turns to a roar.

Silver City, are you the mount of mountains? The mountain is the place of transfiguration. Here one has the possibility of vision that would be aborted or stillborn in the valley. I need the encouragement that comes with the mountain, lest I become locked into a one-dimensional world, the existent.

The mountain is the place of the Law. Here, awareness

of the shoulds, the oughts, is burned into the hardness of our consciousness.

The mountain is also the place of the Sermon. Here the essence of ethics is received. Here is heard the summation of the way to live.

Concretely, while I am here, I read Dostoevsky and Teilhard, F. Scott Fitzgerald and Jacques Ellul and Viktor Frankl, Willi Marxsen on *The Resurrection of Jesus of Nazareth* and Willie Morris's *The Last of the Southern Girls*. Also Mark Twain's autobiography. I do not open the day with the *Los Angeles Times* and close it with Walter Cronkite. I miss them, but I do not really want them here.

There is the change in diet, now much simpler, prepared over a wood fire outside the cabin or on a gas stove that performs spasmodically. Meals become an occasion for community, not just in the breaking of bread, but in all the attendant labors of preparation and cleanup, so different from the modern kitchen.

When we turn to late-night conversation, there are new depths. Here, there has been time for the first time for my daughter to realize what it will mean to soon leave home, to go for her senior year of high school in Sweden. Her dawning awareness brings tears. I feel those tears, and they feel good. Being torn between holding to what we have known and moving to a new situation is something we have all experienced. For her, it is the most encompassing of all the departures she has contemplated.

Mostly, there is time to think.

There is the temptation to want to stay in Silver City. The urge away from work and home is finally fulfilled, but the temptation passes. Strange as it may seem, by the end of my stay, I am restless to return to the valley. Why have I here so little in common with the three who wanted to stay?

As I come, as I stay, as I leave, I am aware that the mountain is not just the place of Transfiguration, of Law, of the Sermon. It is also one of the places of Temptation. It is the will to power, the infatuation with authority. After all, it is the place to play King of the Hill. Away from people, the Tempter speaks of power over them. Even here at Silver City the Tempter comes. He comes because I am here.

°⟦People⟧°

*Outwardly, he was a defeated man. Maybe it was the De-*pression. More likely, it was his wife. She would have defeated any man. They were both old from the time I first knew them. She wanted to adopt me, and as with every determination of hers, he complied. Dad, or Pete as he was known to the world, bore his fate in silence. Oh, he could talk. He could swear with feeling and creativity. I have never known his match in swearing. And when he was in a group of men only, his tongue would loosen. As a small boy, I loved to sit around the edge and listen to stories he told of earlier exploits with threshing crews, horses, and men. But with the family, he managed only minimal replies.

I liked him, and I liked to be with him. He had an inner strength. He also had a physical strength, even with his years, of which I stood in awe. To be with him in caring for the cattle or in making hay or fixing fences was deeply satisfying. Then I felt like a *man*. Perhaps the most treasured time of my youth was out in the timber with him,

27

cutting black jacks (a scrub oak) for firewood. Rarely did we speak. We simply cut away with the axes, downing trees, trimming them, and burning the brush. Still I had a sense of just being with him.

He even treated me like a man, usually. The women were always fearful for me, always trying to protect me, but he let me go, let me do, and let me learn for myself. He also let me get out of my own trouble. I remember once being in the field with him. We were harrowing with a team of four horses. After he started the job, he let me take the team while he sat in the shade of a locust grove. On about the second round, nearly a half-mile away from where he was sitting, when I came to the end of the field, I turned the team too short and upset the harrow, putting it on top of me. The harness of the horses became all tangled, and things were generally in a mess. The bruises and cuts created less pain than the awareness of the stupidity of what I had done. It took me a long time to get the harrow and the team back in order. All the time, I kept looking at that grove of trees, hoping Dad might not have seen it happen, hoping I could get everything back in order without his knowing or at least without his help. No movement at the grove! I had made it! When I was finally back where he was sitting, he said nothing. Though my appearance would give evidence that something had happened, I thought I had made it through undetected. Much later, when we stopped for dinner, he managed a remark that let me know he knew. He said simply, "Do you know how to turn a team of horses now?"

He wore blue bib overalls. Dangling from a bib pocket was a tag at the end of a string. The tag belonged to a sack of Golden Grain tobacco. Occasionally, he used Velvet or Prince Albert, but almost exclusively, Golden Grain. With it, he smoked a pipe, and though I was strictly forbidden to smoke, his pipe always had an appeal for me— even today this fascination with pipes has not faded. As a small boy, I often had earache. The pain was soothed by his blowing smoke into my ear. Several times, I recall, this happened in the middle of the night.

Although Dad smoked a pipe, he would receive at Christmas or on Father's Day, from his adult children, a box of cigars. He kept the cigars in the kitchen cabinet, and as he slowly smoked them, perhaps two or three a week, I would sneak one out and smoke it. I tried to be careful not to take too many, lest he notice them missing. Now I realize he must have known that I was taking them, but he never said a word about it, and he never changed the place where he kept them. I think I would never be able to let something like that pass as he did.

Mom, or "Aunt Doll" as she was known to the world, was a despot. Her word was law. It was spoken with authority. Her adult children, five of them, stood in fear of her. The neighbors trembled in the face of her anger, and I was afraid. Her sharp tongue made her a character in the community. Sometimes, like once at an auction, I overheard people talking about her. When visitors came to the farm to do business, they talked with her. She did the banking. She made the decisions. I always hoped that Dad would stand up to her, demand to have a say in things, but he never did.

Now I look back upon her as colorful. She was *somebody*. But then it was no fun. At home I had to endure, and away from home, I was embarrassed for people to know that I belonged to her.

Yet beyond this harsh exterior were traits of kindness and generosity. For example, she had compassion for animals. She would permit only a straight bit in the mouths of the horses because other bits could hurt them. It did not matter that a boy or even a man could not really control a determined horse with just a straight bit.

One time I was sent on horseback to a neighbor's a half mile away. I was to get a dozen eggs and was given a gallon syrup-bucket in which to carry them. On the way back, something happened to make the horse give a quick jump. That made the eggs rattle in the can. The noise scared the horse more, and he began to run. He was a big horse, and with a straight bit, I could not hold him. The more he ran, the more the eggs rattled, sending him faster. I arrived home with a dozen liquid eggs. Immediately I was sent back, this time with a paper sack, and I returned with nobler results.

Horses were not to be whipped and not to be run. They did get run, out of her sight, but if they came back in a lather of sweat and breathing hard, there was a reckoning.

Often a sow's litter of pigs would have a runt or two that could not survive if left with the sow. These runts were brought into the house and nursed, fed with a bottle, until they could make it outside. Once when I was about fourteen, I learned that a certain neighbor was coming. There was the possibility that her daughter, the same age as I, might also come. I had fantasies of this girl being my girl friend, and the few times I had been near her, her looks and smiles had not discouraged that idea. They did come. In anticipation, I washed and combed my hair to look my best, but just as mother and daughter arrived at the door, one little pig that had been cared for in the house ran out of the kitchen onto the big cement step. Having diarrhea, as often happened with these bottle-fed pigs, he squirted a stream all over that step. My humiliation was complete. I knew the chances for love or any respect in the eyes of that girl were gone. I evaporated as quickly as I could. Later when we went to high school together, she was kind enough never to mention that episode.

Mom's kindness led her to rescue me from an orphan's home. Today people adopt children to enlarge their own lives. While they no doubt have the welfare of the child in mind, that is not their dominant motivation. Then orphans were looked upon more as objects of charity. In taking me, she was doing a good work. Had there been all the home-study procedures in effect then as now, she would never have made it. By age, she and Dad were too old. Their relationship was not exactly intimate—they did not share the same bedroom; if they rode in a car together, it was in different seats. Financially, they could not have passed the test. Fortunately for me, things had not yet become civilized for social workers.

Being an orphan was not easy, and it was not made more palatable by "Little Orphan Annie," whom I have always detested. The kids at school used to tease me by calling me by my name prior to adoption. There was just no way to escape that status. When visitors came, the folks would introduce me as "our adopted son." Finally one day when guests were gone, I whimpered, "Why do you always have to say 'our *adopted* son?'"

One of Mom's daughters was there at the time, and she laughed, saying, "But Mom, people will know you're too old to have a child that age."

To which she sharply retorted, "I'll show them!" She

was then, I think, in her midfifties. Never again was I introduced as an adopted child.

Mom had certain teachings that were delivered over and over again and were understood. One has stayed with me: "If you say you'll do a thing, do it if it kills you." My church presents this teaching in a more genteel form: "A Brethren's word is as good as his bond." She taught that, and she held me to it. Two or three times I used it against her. When I asked to go somewhere, and the answer was no, I protested, "But I told such and such a person I would be there," which I had, anticipating the need for such an argument. And it worked! But after the second or third time, she added a measure to the teaching, "You had better be a little more careful what you promise!" That I understood also and did not again exploit that situation. Ingrained in me still is the necessity to make good on what I say I will do.

Many times I suffered from whippings. Probably all of them were deserved, but at the time, through my tears, I felt the gravest injustice had been done. I plotted ways to get even or to make her feel sorry for what she had done. As I grew older, I learned that Mom's most vulnerable time was right after she had whipped me. Then was the time to ask for what might ordinarily be denied.

The one who really took responsibility for caring for me was Edith. She was a daughter who had never married, and she made life bearable. She had a measure of softness which was a rare ingredient in that environment. She cared for me, made my clothes, kept me clean, and pleaded my cause. And it was she who bore the hurt that comes in living with the antagonisms and spitefulness of an adolescent. She did it with grace. Without her, I think I could not have survived.

"I'm so happy you belong to the Lord." An elderly woman, her face lined deeply with life, said that to me a few years ago as I was flying to Birmingham, Alabama. Sitting beside me in the plane, she noticed that I was reading a book "about Paul." That initiated our conversation, during which she later asked about my work. At that time I was serving as a denominational staff member. She was greatly pleased when I agreed that it was "something like a preacher." Her parting words were those quoted at the beginning, and a deep joy underscored them.

How in contrast was the reaction of a man a few hours earlier upon seeing the same book. He was an effusive, outwardly jovial, and urbane man. Both of us had experienced flight cancellations and were at the airline counter trying to make some alternative arrangement. Spotting the book in my hand, he casually asked what I was reading. Then he slowly read the title, *More Preaching Values in the Epistles of Paul*. He looked up at me with an expression that seemed to say, "What's the matter with you?" His whole demeanor changed; gone was the joviality, and I thought how different this would have been had I been reading *The Status Seekers* or *I, the Jury*. No doubt, there was an opportunity in that situation for a witness, but I am afraid I missed it.

A woman of middle years has epilepsy. She also has a sadness of the soul: "My children don't want me around. They wish I were dead." Sad, yet even sadder are those situations when parents give birth to unwanted children.

The prisoner sitting across from me was obviously enjoying himself. A few minutes before, his parole officer had told me that I would be his *first* visitor in some forty years. Nine years old when his police record began, he was then in his sixties. Soon he would be considered for parole, and while he had failed every other time upon release, he said, "I want just one more chance to show that there's a little bit of good in old Joe."

Joe Levy was recognized as one of the top con artists in the country. Writing worthless checks was just one of the offenses that had placed him in the federal penitentiary at Leavenworth.

Joe got his one more chance. The Church of the Brethren in Kansas City, Kansas, with a sense of responsibility to a man who had had so little befriending, arranged for him a job and housing. He began a new life. In less than two weeks, Joe was nowhere to be found. He had skillfully passed a number of checks. He had shown the world that there was more than just a little bit left in the professional skills he had developed over a lifetime.

The church failed? No. They were not called to succeed with the man. They were called to give themselves.

Oral Roberts makes an interesting observation in his autobiography, *My Story*. (This book was offered to us free of charge after a visit to his headquarters in Tulsa. Naturally, we accepted. There are two things one ought never to refuse—a free book and a free cup of coffee. Incidentally, Mr. Roberts declares that God told him to build that headquarters building. Considering the lavish and exotic woods and stones used in the construction, God must have been in an extravagant mood that day.) He calls it "my great discovery" when he saw clearly "that God is good, that he wants only good to come to his children. I saw that God wanted to heal and bless people, while the devil wanted to oppress and destroy them."

Ultimately, God's goodness must be affirmed, else it leaves us only with a spiritual self-flagellation. But the road to "ultimately" is pitted with such things as Golgotha and a tentmaker's "thorn in the flesh."

Diana Barrymore wrote about herself. She was thirty-five years old, and having everything, she had nothing. The daughter of John Barrymore, she was born into beauty and wealth and privilege, but in a black-jacketed book published in 1957 and titled *Too Much, Too Soon*, she revealed a self-tragedy of immorality, degradation, and addiction.

Three years later, she lay dead, cut down by alcohol and sleeping pills. It was a postscript to that widespread impulse, "I don't want my children to struggle the way I have had to do."

From his first "Can I he'p ya?" to his parting slur at the "happy pappies" (trainees in the federal poverty program), Ranger John gave us a unique experience with humanity.

We saw him but two weeks. We were in Pineville State Park in Kentucky, up five beautiful miles of mountainside near the Cumberland Gap.

John, in appearance and language completing the image of the fabled mountaineer, was the park ranger who assigned spaces for trailers and tents and collected the fees. "You know what's wrong with this place?" John asked us soon after the first night's sandwiches and potato chips were finished, "It's them damned old Republicans and Baptist preachers. They ganged up to get prohibition in this here county. Some days it's dry as a bone up here—can't find a hit anywhere." I'm sure he shared this bit of information just in case we might offer that which would quench his thirst.

While John was suspicious of the Democrats and their war on poverty because it brought wages higher than men were receiving in the lumber mills, he reserved hatred for the Republicans: "The Lord is kinder to dogs than he is to Republicans! He opens the dogs' eyes in nine days, but he ain't never opened the Republicans' eyes."

"I've read the Bible through three times," he once told us. (He told another family that it was seven times. Talk about speed reading!) And he could quote Scripture as avidly as he could swear, both flowing freely as he entered intensely into "religious" dialogue. But in what he said there was seriousness and there was common sense. He was not misled by rabble radio. "Did you ever hear that ol' Carl McIntire?" he asked us.

"Yes," we said, wondering if John might be his disciple. "What do you think of him?" we asked.

"He ought to be tuk out and strung up to the first maple. He's just tryin' to get people's money and they

36

ain't bright enuf to see it. He wants you to give it to him instead of your own preacher, and he throws in that Communist junk just to scare folks. I always believe in payin' my own preacher, then I know where it goes."

Among the rumors about John was the report that he had killed the father of his first wife. She had not been understanding about this and divorced him. He had remarried, and some said he also had a mistress.

John seldom went to church, he said, even though "they called me to preach one time. But the Lord didn't call me. When the Lord calls a man to preach, you know it!" He did not go because people looked at him "funny" and talked about his being divorced and having a second wife. "Those Baptists just don't understand forgiveness. When the Lord promises to forgive, he don't mean maybe. He means everything—completely. He don't hold back on nothing."

Amazing grace.

"Git away from that water!" With that sharp command, I was introduced to Mary Frances Zadora. She was not yelling at me but at a blond-haired boy, a scant two years old, clad only in once-white shorts covering essentials but drooping to his knees. His forbidden play area was the water spigot for two rows of tiny houses at the Osceola Housing Project for migrants, Belle Glade, Florida. I was there to learn what I could about the church's ministry to migrants.

Interesting woman, Mrs. Zadora. I asked if the boy was her son. "No," she said, "he belongs to my neighbors, and

I'm takin' care of the little devil while she gone shoppin'."
Did she have any children? Only one, and "he ain't right
bright." Further conversation established that he was in an
institution for mentally retarded children. I questioned
whether she knew that President Kennedy had had a sister
with a similar problem. She did not answer immediately.
After a long drag on her cigarette, she finally spoke, looking away into the distance, not about her child, but about
the president. "That was too bad about Kennedy, but I
guess it was just his time to go."

Robert and Mary Frances Zadora lived in a tin building
about twelve feet by twenty feet, one of about 140 such
buildings in the migrant camp. It rented for four dollars
a week. There was one room, no plumbing; light was
from a single bulb dangling from the center of the room.
There was better housing in Belle Glade, but the cost was
more and the waiting list long.

When Robert joined his wife on the porch, I asked if I
might take a picture of them. Grinning, she said, "Lord,
it might break the camera." But they were willing, even
eager, to be photographed though somewhat aware that
their appearance was less than ideal. "If you was here
yesterday, you couldn't have took no picture," Mrs.
Zadora told me. "I danced all night Saturday night till I
couldn't even stand up."

The late Ed Murrow called it a "Harvest of Shame."

Having been raised in the Southwest, I was always just
a little suspicious of Roy Rogers. His clothes, or something

38

about him, just did not look like the cowhands I knew. Maybe it was the clean hat or the fancy pants.

Still, who would not be impressed with the way he handles a six-gun. A plaster ball is thrown high into the air. Quick is the draw! Fast and sure the aim! Rogers's trusty six-shooter punctures another ball in flight! Anyone who has ever tried to pierce a swiftly moving object with a bullet knows that it takes "some shootin'."

Then one day I read about this little trick. Instead of a regular bullet, the cartridge is filled with fine buckshot, and when fired, they scatter over an area of five or six feet. If Rogers gets the gun out of the holster, he practically can't miss.

In my job, I sometimes wish for hidden buckshot.

They came to this country as refugees. He was from the Netherlands, she, from Indonesia. He had been in the Dutch army in Indonesia, married her, and they became unacceptable in either Indonesia or the Netherlands as the Dutch were expelled from their former colonial holding.

Our church, near Lawrence, Kansas, sponsored them. What a surprise it had been to the church when she arrived and was Oriental in appearance! It was a growing experience for the congregation to accept that interracial marriage.

My wife and I were in their living room shortly after they arrived. He and I, a few days before, had spent a successful day finding him employment as a parts manager in an auto agency. The house in which they were living had been prepared by members of the church. Many of them had given items of furniture or food, but sitting there, I felt the house still looked rather bare.

The small, gracious Indonesian lady, knowing scarcely a word of English, served us tea. She used a tea warmer in preparing it. The warmer was something we had not seen before, and we remarked about it. Later, as we were ready to leave, the couple insisted that we take it with us. We declined, not wanting to take from a family who seemed to have so little and especially not something like this tea warmer from Indonesia which they could not replace.

They insisted, saying, "The church and you have given us much. Now it is our turn. We would like to give also."

We received their gift and treasured it. Perhaps we realized as not before that all people need to be able both to give and to receive and that gifts can be offered out of meagerness as well as surplus.

He was an alcoholic, and he found strength in saying that. For a time, I worked beside him in a printing plant in Lawrence, Kansas. It seemed strange to me at first that day after day he would relate the story of his dissipation, wallowing in a mire of alcoholism only to find the under-girding and support of other alcoholics in Alcoholics Anonymous. AA had helped him pull himself from the gutter. The repetition of the stories came with such regularity that in time I came to feel I could tell them as well as he.

He had difficulty sleeping at night. I understand this is not unusual for alcoholics. To fill these endless hours of wakefulness, he went near and far to AA meetings. One evening, he took me with him to Topeka for a meeting of alcoholics gathered from a wide area. This was my first encounter with this remarkable organization. The meeting, once under way, had a tang of familiarity; people were standing to testify to their victory over alcohol and to what the twelve steps had done for them. It was a multiplication of what I had been hearing day after day at work.

It bears some similarity to the church. There is a recalling of what, by grace, has happened in the lives of people. There is a body of doctrine which acts as a creed, but most of all there is a fellowship of suffering. The church is weakest when it neglects to recognize and say the equivalent of "I am an alcoholic." It is weakest when we do not recognize that we depend upon one another.

El McNabb was not a bad sort of man. He just refused to "go forward." In my boyhood years, I occasionally went to revival meetings at a neighboring church where evangelists and local church leaders persisted in trying to lead this one man to the altar. He must have enjoyed the pleading and the cajoling because he was often there. Certainly it is true that the sinners got a great deal more attention than the saved. But with all that effort, El McNabb held out.

Long after I left home, I received word of his death. But there was a note of joy at his passing, for about two weeks prior they had finally led this nearly seventy-year-old man to the altar.

Perhaps even the heavens rejoiced, but there was for me

an edge of sadness. If it were an honest conversion, there is surely something tragic about having arrived at it only at the end of life.

The appointment was confirmed. Harry S Truman would see us at his library. It was 1961, and we then lived on the other side of metropolitan Kansas City from Independence.

How did we get such an appointment? It was through a telephone call to the library. I gave my name, residence, and occupation. The appointment was much easier to make than many of those I have made with self-important people who advertise their importance by being too busy to see you.

My wife and I and our three children were ushered into his office. He greeted us cordially and sat down to talk concerning those matters in which we had interest. Now, just what was it we wanted to talk to him about? What does one talk about to a man who has been president and with whom you have had no previous acquaintance? Conversation was not easy, did not feel natural, and was not particularly engaging—though he was an engaging man. I did recall with him that, while in the Marine Corps, I had on occasions guarded him at the presidential camp near Thurmont, Maryland (later to be called Camp David).

Our first glimpse of him was a little startling because he had aged more than we realized and was not as steady as we had expected from seeing him in news photos. Still he had the tang and saltiness for which he was famous.

With some hesitation, I had brought along a camera. As our visit was closing, I asked if I might take a picture of him with my children. He simply snorted, "Huh, you can if you don't think it'll hurt them!" And when they stood beside him, he said to my wife, "Get over here, young lady, you're in this, too."

A brief glimpse of a man to whom the years since his departure from office have been kind in gathering affection and respect.

Joseph. He was a Muhammad Ali in the days when the boxer was Cassius Clay shouting, "I am the greatest." He was a Joe Namath, conceited and arrogant, yet handsome and irresistible, even to the older ladies. Joseph had something attractive about him, and it was not Hai Karate. He was a Henry Kissinger who, while not the head of state, was his chief advisor and exercised great power as he predicted the future, as he laid plans to meet the crises of the country.

And the vote was ten to one for his death.

Clarence Darrow. I respond to his life and most of what he represented, even as I disagree with much that he said.

Darrow was a successful railroad corporation lawyer when at the age of thirty-seven he quit that job to defend Eugene Debs and the striking Pullman workers. From that time until his death at eighty years of age in 1938, he became recognized as a great criminal lawyer who defended the famous, the outcast, the nameless, the helpless, the criminal. My impression is that he did not enjoy public approval in his lifetime. If you read what the newspapers of that day said about him, you will find it not flattering.

I have problems with Darrow. To begin with, he was a militant agnostic. He even went on the Chautauqua circuit to debate some of what Christianity was teaching. He did not believe in the divinity of Jesus, and he could not understand God as either a personal being or as a creator.

The primary acquaintance of a younger generation with Darrow has been through the play *Inherit the Wind*. It was made into a movie in which Spencer Tracy gave a marvelous performance in the role of Darrow. The play is about the Scopes trial in Tennessee where a young teacher was being tried for violation of a law against teaching evolution. Like drama must do, the play depends upon fiction as well as fact. Unfortunately, the play makes a fool of William Jennings Bryan in the courtroom. Bryan was enlisted by the prosecution and was Darrow's opponent in the trial. In the play, Bryan and religious sentiment at the time are drawn in caricature. He appears ridiculous, and no rational person would identify with him in the contest with Darrow. In the actual trial, Darrow lost, Bryan won. Scopes was convicted, but such was Darrow's effectiveness on behalf of freedom and justice that in losing, he won. Scopes got a minor sentence, but the verdict was later reversed on a technicality by the Tennessee Supreme Court.

Despite my admiration for Darrow, I cannot now celebrate with glee his victory. Once I would have been more excited about it, but Bryan spoke a line in the heat of debate on evolution that has given me pause. He said, "I am more interested in the Rock of Ages than in the age of rocks." On that priority, I must stand with Bryan, not with Darrow. Let me look foolish and ignorant, I stand there.

Darrow defended Loeb and Leopold after they had killed the boy, Bobby Franks. The public outcry for the execution of these wealthy and brilliant young men was great. Darrow did not declare their innocence but had them plead guilty. Then he begged for their lives, pleaded that they not be hung. His oratory in their defense is one of the great pieces of literature of the time. He was successful. Small wonder that Nathan Leopold, a Jew, would write in his life's story, *Life Plus 99 Years*, "If I were asked to name two men who, in my opinion, came closest to preaching the pure essence of love—love for the human race—I think I'd feel compelled to name Jesus of Nazareth and Clarence Darrow."

But the defense which Darrow presented for the two young men is very different from my own understanding. I can applaud his defending their lives. I can applaud his opposition to capital punishment. But when he defends Loeb and Leopold on the basis of a form of insanity, saying that if you had known everything about their past, you would know why they could do no other than they did—that argument takes away their freedom of action. That takes away man as we have understood him in creation. He becomes a creature determined by forces over which he has no control. That is not a picture of man as given by Joshua in his charge to Israel, "Choose this day whom you will serve" (Josh. 24:15).

Still, I am moved by Darrow's defense. He was torn as to whether he should accept the assignment or not. He was sixty-eight years old, and he wrote in his autobiography that, at the time, "I had grown tired of standing in the lean and lonely front line facing the greatest enemy that ever confronted man—public opinion." But he believed that "in a terrible crisis, there is only one element more helpless than the poor, and that is the rich."

Some of Darrow's attraction for me, I think, is revealed in what he wrote of himself toward the end of his life in his *The Story of My Life*. He said, "I had stood with the hunted for many years. I had fought against hatred, passion, and vengeance to save liberty and life, and I was weary, and timorous of the crowd. It was hard to longer brace myself for the fray. . . . So I determined to close my office door and call it my day's work. Or a life work. . . . I was seventy-two years old, and it was high time that I should begin to stroll peacefully and pleasantly toward the end of the trail which, at best, must be a little way beyond."

"I had stood with the hunted." That is the key to my attraction. That is why I would stand with him.

⚬[Definings]⚬

Love begins with impulse, for impulse is the embryo of feeling, and in feeling there is imagination. Only when you have felt despair can you imagine what it feels like to someone else. Only when you have felt embarrassment in a situation can you imagine how that feels to someone else. Only when you have felt accepted and loved can you imagine what that means to your neighbor. Imagination is essential to love.

Love begins with impulse, with feeling, but not just any impulse or feeling. Love has boundaries; it is not like the rampaging Mississippi at flood, flowing anywhere and everywhere, caring not where it spreads. Tolstoy talked about the Russian ladies who went to the theater and cried with great emotion but gave no thought to their own coachmen sitting outside in the freezing cold. Love is not haphazard or erratic. It does not come with smooth butter one moment and bring a sharp gouge the next.

Love begins with impulse, but it moves with calmness. Love can be calm because it is not threatened. A person who loves has accepted himself. He loves himself in fulfilling the teaching of Jesus that we are to love our neighbors as we love ourselves; we cannot love others if we hate ourselves. Love can be expressed when we are secure enough about who we are to give attention beyond ourselves. Love is not self-conscious. We forget self for the time. We lose that kind of self-awareness that makes it impossible for us to think about anyone or anything else.

Those persons from whom I have experienced love were those who were free to express interest and love because they did not need always to be gathering significance for themselves. Perhaps they were secure enough in their own ideas that they could be interested in mine.

Love begins with impulse. It moves with calmness. It ends in creativity, for it brings into being that which had not been.

Worship is recalling God's action in the history of his people and in our personal experience. It is remembering God's promises and the fulfillment of those promises. It is celebrating past and present reality and future hope. It is exploring God's will for our lives and for the life of his people and for the world. Worship is the central experience that brings together the people of God.

Prayer is awareness of a power that is beyond you. Prayer is being open to God's influence upon your thinking. Prayer is love received and love expressed. Prayer is deepening the intensity of your intention. Prayer is acknowledging your own limitations and needs. Prayer is genuine concern about your family and your neighbor. Prayer is concentration which replaces fleeting and fragmentary thoughts about what your life means. Prayer is spontaneous expression not curbed by the judgments and expressions of other people. Prayer is the means of enriching life, of realizing the gathering and growing of life. Prayer is mobilizing our resources for justice and peace and mercy. Prayer is a distant gaze, a bowed head, a bent knee, a time of stillness, a chord of music, a smile, a tear, aloneness, closeness with others, most of all, a rhythm of meditation and action.

Christians are a people more identified with a vision than with a doctrine. That does not mean we have no solid teachings or firm understandings to share. It does mean that those doctrines become the substance of a dream which we declare.

The difference between a Christian and a non-Christian is not that they are in separate worlds. It is in the way they understand and experience events and their vision of what is coming.

Excuses are the termites of character, the acid that cankers the bond of friendship. Excuses are the graveyard of opportunity, the booby traps on the road to the New

Jerusalem. Excuses are missed free-throws. Excuses are to faith as a cat is to a canary.

As for the excuses that are given for noninvolvement in the church, about 90 percent of them are one of these:

I am too busy!
Sunday is the only day I have to rest.
The church is full of hypocrites.
My parents forced me to go to church when I was a child.

They are hard to take seriously. It would be much more satisfying to meet the deeper objection or the honest doubt.

Sin is thought to be a rouged woman, selling her body in Beirut or on Times Square. Sin is thought to be a massage parlor in Berkeley. Sin is thought to be taking heroin or smoking pot. Sin is thought to be a leering ad for the movie that promises Scandinavian sex. Sin is thought to be alcohol and tobacco and free love. Sin is thought to be gambling, Las Vegas at night, getting something for nothing. Sin is thought to be stealing, whether taking by gun or by deception.

Hah! If only sin were so simple, so manageable, so external. These things do reflect a brokenness in man, more to be met with pity and pathos than with revenge and punishment.

Sin is a deeper condition. It comes to us in dullness, in loss of nerve, in maintained, controlled anger. It comes to us in loneliness when we have only ourselves.

✻

Fear is the beginning, the first emotion of faith. It is what shepherds felt when first they saw the glory of God. It was fear that filled them when first they heard the good news. Augustine spoke of fear as the needle, sharp and painful, but bringing in the thread that will form the union between man and his Maker.

Fear is the beginning. It reveals a yearning. It wishes for something else. Fear prompts us to withhold, to probe, to change our relations with others. It is a warning that helps us avoid the sledgehammer that can destroy new and tender connections. Fear makes it hard for us to speak to an assembly and sometimes to a committee of five, but that very fear also tells us that it is worthwhile, that it means something. When fear is missing, so is excitement and intensity. When fear is missing, a part of life has been ripped away.

Fear is one of the elements of creaturehood that puts us in touch with the whole of creation.

But there is another side to fear. Fear is a fearful thing if it stays. Fear puts men under white sheets and sends them burning crosses. Fear recruits for the John Birch Society. Fear sets the torch to Watts and Chicago's west side. Fear crushes the petals of personality. Fear sends people to the sports shops to buy handguns, and fear pulls the trigger. Fear worries about property values when there is the possibility of a new kind of neighbor. Fear leaves a youth lonely and isolated. Fear keeps a person quiet on conviction, lest there be a charge of being unpatriotic.

Faith begins in fear but must turn to song if it is to take root and live.

Call a man a prophet and his chest expands, his head lifts, and he moves from back on his heels to place more weight on the balls of his feet. Call him a prophet and you have complimented him, placing him in heroic company— Nathan confronting David, Jeremiah imprisoned in a cistern, Amos lashing the fat heifers of his day, John the Baptist rough in dress and speech, Martin Luther King, Jr., walking the streets with glass and cans and spit hurled at him. Call him a prophet and you have identified him with truth; you have also said that you recognize in him that which is coming.

The prophet has done well without a press agent, without a campaign staff. His image stands as a polished knight —oh, not to all his contemporaries; only later does the prophet become clearly validated in the minds of people.

Call a man a priest, and unless he is that by profession, his chest sinks, his eyes lower, and he looks for a place to sit down. The priest could use a press agent.

⸪〚Interpretings〛⸪

The measure of a man is not whether he is broken or not, but whether he is willing to be broken.

As a lad, I occasionally went to a little neighboring Church of the Nazarene only a short distance from our farm. Once when I was there, they were in a lively revival meeting, and the evangelist used Noah as his subject matter. He proceeded to pound home a parallel between the Noah episode and the destruction that is soon to come upon sinners.

"Did you know," he asked midway, "that in recent days the ark has been found underneath layers and layers of snow and ice high in the mountains of Siberia?" To me, there was something remarkably vivid and threatening about that report. What had been just another Old Testament story had sudden spine-tingling reality. In those moments, I would have hidden behind the pew lest God see me and destroy me even as he did the other sinners in the time of Noah.

The years have made me jaded. Each year I expect reports of the discovery of the ark on some faraway mountain. The threat of God's wrath still scares me, but somehow the ark reports no longer bring awareness of that threat.

There has been no objective reason for us to keep our dog. It has been an act of love. Indeed, it has intimations of grace, for he has absolutely no merits of his own. Revelation speaks of those beyond the gates of the Holy City: "Outside are the dogs and sorcerers and fornicators and murderers and idolaters, and every one who loves and practices falsehood" (Rev. 22:15). Yes, that is the place for our dog. He would feel very much at home in such a company.

He came to us because he was abandoned as a small puppy. When you become acquainted with him, you understand why he was abandoned. Anyway, my wife and I were in Mississippi when a telephone call home advised us of this addition to our family. Having been rather conventional in naming our children, I wanted to become a connoisseur in christening the animal. Why not a name, I thought, sounding a bit wickedly foreign? Let the name end in *i;* let it be a name never before borne by a dog. But other values intervened. Surely the children should have a chance to help name him. They were not particularly enamored with the idea of some strange-sounding appellation, and they placed upon him the title *Friskie.* That's not exactly letting imagination run wild! Still it fit, in a strange way, for he has always been given to frolic, and not of the gentle sort. He has always been rough. With no outward stimulus, he has been given to racing off through the house at top speed or to weird, distorted movements.

I said he had no merit. In fairness, that is an overstatement but only microscopically so. While his personal life-style has been rough, as regards others, he is a pacifist. He has never wanted fighting among the children or even loud, harsh speaking at one another. When a scuffle begins, even in light fun, Friskie gets in the middle of it, barking, jumping against the people, and threatening them until it stops.

He is a law-and-order dog—for others. For his own behavior, he chooses evil and disorder. Leave a door ajar, and he speeds for it—freedom and love. He is highly motivated by love. He knows how to take the heat. In fact, he has not waited for the open door, he has clawed and torn open the screens in order to get away.

Some of his characteristics could not be called evil, I think, because they are not volitional. For example, I doubt that he consciously sheds hair; but nonetheless he is a prodigious hair producer and shedder. Where he sits, he leaves a cushion. Where he walks or runs, a cloud of hair fogs outward from all around him for three or four inches. There is one plus to all this: intimacy. When we leave the house, people always come near us to pick off the dog hair.

Another thing quite beyond his control. We left him one summer in the care of a young girl. She, having things of great moment to command her attention, left him tied too long in the sun. His whole back became a giant blister, and he almost died. His death at that point would have saved us years of suffering. He was nursed back to life, but since then, he regularly has convulsions. At such times, he becomes not only convulsively out of control, but also sick, so that he loses what he has eaten. Occasionally, we are lucky and get him outside before that happens.

Once, the school summer program was having a dog show. Some neighbor boys, not having a dog themselves, came to ask if they could borrow Friskie for the show. Permission granted. They returned with a red ribbon! He had won second prize for "best markings," whatever that means. Anyway, for a time we looked at him in a new light, with almost a glint of pride, as our "prize-winning" dog.

Oh, yes, perhaps you could call it a merit that he loves to play. He is good at keep-away when two people are throwing a ball back and forth between them. He is less skilled when he goes to the outside. He plays hide-and-seek. He has assorted tricks performed best for our daughter, who has been his mentor.

That's the way Friskie is, but we keep him. He is part of our life. He has accepted the way we are; we have tried to do as much for him.

More and more, I am impressed with the unfairness and the utter inequality life deals us. Why should a president who is young, full of vigor and vision, suddenly have life snatched away? Why can some people make and hold friends easily while others are shunned? Why can some present their arguments so convincingly while others cannot even get a hearing? Why does cancer take the life of a mother who has three small children and leave another untouched? Why do gifts tend to be concentrated so that a person able to do one thing well will likely also be able to do the other thing? While I know there are some things I can do, I am typically more aware of what I cannot do. When I see gifts in art and music and speaking or in just handling a situation, I become overwhelmed with what some can do. When I realize my own capacity in such a context, it becomes depressing.

The world is not fair. It is not equal. To hang around with that thought too long is to have a bad companion. To try to resolve it or to justify it is an exercise in self-destruction. So with such thought, I try to be casual and to leave before I become immersed.

A lay leader was showing a youth group through the church and describing the life of the church which was a bit different from our own. They had no ministers, the lay leader explained. They do have preaching, but the lay-man who speaks on a given Sunday never knows ahead of time the subject on which he will be preaching. He simply goes to the pulpit Bible, opens it, and begins to read and comment at the place where it falls open.

This is the greatest labor-saving plan for preaching that has been revealed to man.

Paul, or whoever it was penned the missive to Titus, declared that a bishop, "as God's steward, must be blameless"

(Tit. 1:7). Now that is a screening process that, if taken seriously and literally, would greatly thin the ranks of the bishopric.

In days past, one of the first prayers taught to little children was:

> Now I lay me down to sleep,
> I pray Thee, Lord, my soul to keep;
> If I should die before I wake,
> I pray Thee, Lord, my soul to take.

I learned but do not recall using this prayer in my own childhood. I do remember the great relief felt many times at just being alive the next day. After a day of badness, I was glad just to be alive. I knew that had I died during the night I would have gone to hell for certain. This fear of what God would do with me was uncomfortable though it was not altogether effective in shaping my thoughts and activities.

When I read about that woman who wasted ointment on Jesus' head, when I think of its value and Jesus' response, I ponder whether my giving, my faith response, may not be too realistic, measured, and calculated.

I confess that I do not find great comfort in reading church ads. Indeed, there is discomfort, and it is not primarily with those that use hell as do the movie ad-copy writers. No, there is greater problem with those ads that promise to do something for you. They offer God as your servant. He will get rid of your guilt, budge out your grudge, make you feel young and happy. It is as if they have called God into service and they now offer him to serve you also.

Some draw cartoons of the church, painting it as a cranky old woman with fire in her eyes and her mouth turned down at the corners. The church is painted as caricature Puritan, without humor or flesh.

Well, it may be that the church has sometimes misunderstood and thought that God sent us to judge the world. My impression is, however, that in our time we have erred on the other side. That is, we have been so eager to accept anything and everybody that we have not offered a vision of what life might be.

One wonders what Peter's response would have been had it been suggested to him that the vow of chastity was necessary for him to fulfill his religious vocation.

Private zone. Do not enter. The geography of the closed door is very important. It must erect a temporary wall or a wide chasm that separates us from others into our aloneness. It may be at late evening, walking along the beach when the bikinis and the sunburned skins have gone, and you see and hear only the rhythm of the ocean reaching out and falling back. It may be in the early morning sunlight, filtering through the trees, high in the mountains, drinking a cup of coffee, smelling the pine, and with no place to go for hours. It may be in the middle of the day, in a platform rocker in a bedroom, with a book—not a book that you race through but one that must be read slowly and reread to digest, then a sentence interrupts your reading and sends your mind out exploring something you had never thought about before. That book will sometimes be the Good Book, and there it becomes the Living Word.

The geography is important. It must be away from the telephone, blessing though the telephone otherwise is for communication. It must be away from babies who are crying for diapers to be changed. It must be away from teenagers forcing you to make a decision about whether they can go somewhere or not. It must be away from parents who remind you of what you have not done, away from the talk and demands of husband or wife and away from the noise of engines and electronic media. Sometime during the day, the week, the year, the soul needs to rest from all that noise and all those people.

In our aloneness is time to heal, meditate, create.

A couple flirt with the end of their relationship. Their communication becomes hard; their words are aimed at barbing as much as carrying the most meager message. Frustration leads them to deny even what has been good. They see the world in two different ways; they both yearn for affection, but they cannot exchange it.

Did you know that the word *disciple* is never mentioned by Paul? Indeed, it is not used outside the Gospels and the Book of Acts, but in these five books it is used about 260 times. That kind of learned data sounds impressive, but it is really not so difficult if you have a concordance or if you happen to come across the fact in a book by William Barclay or some other writer. It may even be helpful information.

Christians never differ, never quarrel, never fight. No. No. Not that. That speaks more of death than life. The difference in faith made alive through discussion and debate, and faith made destructive, is whether those involved enter it feeling fully arrived and needing to convince others, or feeling as pilgrims with other pilgrims, both needing to search to find the way.

Many find themselves on the boundary between secular and sacred. They see values in both but cannot seem to choose.

Secular man has confidence in himself or, if not himself, in his ability to choose and identify experts. Religious man has confidence in God. He chooses to identify with other people in discerning what God is about.

Secular man is a pragmatist. He asks what works. He is determined to make the institution responsible and responsive. Religious man is inclined to ask first what does it mean. To him, there is something more important than whether a thing or an institution works. He asks why. He asks what kind of thing or institution it is. What is it doing?

Secular man's experience has given him confidence in rational proofs and pleasure in the sensitivity circuit. Religious man's experience has given him confidence in revelation, in a body of doctrine and belief, and pleasure in living out what is revealed.

Secular man's jargon is informed by the youth culture and by the recent best sellers. Religious man has a jargon also. It is informed by the fellowship and the all-time best seller.

Secular man has an optimism about himself, about technology, and about the progress of humanity. Religious man has a sense of the tragic. He feels his own brokenness, a brokenness that he cannot expose to the world, that even nags at his relationship to God. He sees progress in mechanics, but he is not so certain about man. He is sober yet hopeful.

No credit accrues to the man who rides in his chariot above the people and above the agony and the pain and the laughter and the joy of life. No credit lies in being in total command of life and every situation. Rather, life at its deepest asks, Are you ready to be vulnerable?

The reason people have difficulty discussing political issues within the context of the church is that they have placed a higher loyalty with a politician than with God; they identify more with a political party than they do with Christ's church; they give a greater place to political philosophy in their lives than they do to the life and message of Jesus Christ.

A piece of candy is nice. So is a bit of fruit punch. But not for long. We can take the sweet for a time, but then it's good to have the biting, the bitter, the sour—the black coffee or the vinegar—to chase away that sweet taste.

So much that has been spoken of love has been done in sweetness. Aldous Huxley's reaction is one we can embrace: "Of all the worn, smudged, dog-eared words in our vocabulary, 'love' is certainly the grubbiest, smelliest, slimiest. Bawled from a million pulpits, lasciviously crooned through hundreds of millions of loudspeakers, it has become an outrage to good taste and decent feeling, an obscenity which one hesitates to pronounce. And yet, it has to be pronounced, for, after all, Love is the last word."

Yes, it must be spoken. With all that is counterfeit and sham, love is still the most beautiful and the most creative of all divine and human acts.

Every journey needs a few signposts. When the destination is love, these five questions may give direction:

1. Can I talk with a person whose morals offend me?
2. Can I describe my neighbor's position so that he will agree that I have stated it fairly?

3. Do I care about what is important to my neighbor?
4. Can I take the first step toward my neighbor?
5. Do I have the impulse to act for my neighbor when I see no immediate gain for myself?

The significance of an event lies in large measure in its anticipation, and in fact a period of anticipation changes the experience of the event itself.

The only rival anticipation has is memory, but memory deals with what has been. Therefore, it cannot be complete as long as life continues. Memory is an off-stage prompter in the drama of anticipation. Memory is the kiln where the bricks of anticipation are fired and made ready for building itself.

Dr. Curtis Bowman believed in faith healing, but you had to talk with him a while to understand what he meant by *faith healing*.

A person related to a patient about to have surgery once asked the doctor if he prayed before surgery.

"What do you mean?" asked Dr. Bowman.

"I mean, do you ask God to guide your hand as you do surgery?"

Dr. Bowman came back, "Do you think he would do that? Do you think he would guide my hand so that I could not make a mistake?"

"Yes," the person replied.

"Then you take the knife and let him guide you."

He did not discount prayer, but neither did he believe God would do his work for him. He believed that God intended him to use and develop his knowledge and abilities.

The people most shocked and disappointed in what they find in the church are those who have moved away from it in spirit and practice. They have left the church, but they expect to find it as it was when they left. Even when people leave the church in anger, or they are critical of what the church is doing or not doing, when they remain outside, their mental image of the church remains set. It is fixed at a certain point in time, and even if the church they castigate is no longer anything like what they knew, they never quite understand or accept that change. They want to hold the idea they have. They cling to an ill-focused snapshot rather than a warm, vibrant body.

We are more attuned to the measure of time than to what is happening in that time. In worship we follow the minute hand more devotedly than the ritual.

We have a programed mind set that is constantly ticking away, conscious of the passage of time. In this preoccupation, we demand instant action, instant gratification. We want the planting and the harvesting with one sweep of the hand. We want instant hamburgers from McDonald's, instant fried chicken from the Colonel. Lipton's tries to sell us a package of soup that we can make in eight seconds.

No wonder baseball is having difficulty as an object of our affection; its slow pace and its lack of promise of a definite cutoff time appeals to a different age.

Timothy Leary, the high priest of drugs, comes home to California and jail. There is a girl with him. She met him two months ago. Unable to reach him, reporters crowd around her—a more ravishing prospect, anyway. She breathes into their microphones that she knows him thoroughly and that he is totally good. She met him two months ago.

Fashionable are those marathon sensitivity weekends. People go and return, assuming they can know someone completely in that span of time.

More perceptive than Leary's friend or the sensitivity fad is that statement by Fyodor Dostoevsky dropped into his novel, *Crime and Punishment:* ". . . to know a man thoroughly, one must deal with him gradually and with circumspection, so as not to be influenced by prejudice, which it may be very difficult afterwards to correct."

Instant replays are good, primarily because they slow the action so that you can see and savor the play.

To be satisfying, most of life must have a time investment. There is something to that observation by Antoine de Saint-Exupéry (in *The Little Prince*), "It is the time you have wasted for your rose that makes your rose so important."

Once I participated in a retreat experience which focused on communication. The design called for us to actually work with various media for communicating the message of the church. Our look was at movies, television, the printed page, mimeographing, preaching, and various other media. Then (as Providence has now revealed we must always do) we divided into small groups to engage in a specific medium for communication.

The group in which I found myself chose graffiti, that profane, earthy scratching on the walls of privies and upon construction fences, the edges of books, and highway signs. Around the room we hung giant press-sheets of paper, and with plastic paints and brushes, with felt-tipped pens, we began to draw pictures and to write those things that each of us felt would convey the gospel message in our kind of world. It was fun! Six or seven of us, some with significant artistic ability, some with virtually none, yet, each working here and then working there around the room, with red and then green and then blue and black.

When we finished, we reflected on that experience in communication. One person, not artistically inclined, spoke of the thrill that came that he could work away right beside two who were artists. The artists had not said, "Now, just a minute, we must lay this whole thing out and do it in just certain ways or it will be wrong."

In that experience, the person was freed from the demands of perfection. He was accepted, and he could communicate because he was accepted. That approach does not create a masterpiece, but it can create communication and personhood.

⟨[Scatterings]⟩

My baptism as a child was in a large stock-tank. At the time, I was younger than I want now to admit. Members of the congregation gathered in the corral and stood all the way around the tank as four or five of us took turns being immersed. It was an experience of closeness rather than being far off and private. As we left the tank, the people sang "O Happy Day." That hymn is not much sung in churches now because it is not quite good enough, but then the people did not realize it was not good enough, and they enjoyed singing it. The last verse begins with a statement that still I could sing if I could sing: "Now rest, my long divided heart."

As a child, one thing that was forever on my list of wants was a pair of cowboy boots. Many men I knew wore them, and I thought they would really look good on me.

Finally, after what seemed a lifetime of dreaming and pleading and then earning, I got a pair. They hurt my feet!

Electricity came to our farm when I was eight or ten. It seemed to dawdle, taking an eternity to come. The old farmhouse must have been wired for months before the power was finally turned on.

The wiring was quite simple. A twisted cord and a lightbulb hung from the center of each room. There were no light fixtures and only two or three plug-in sockets in the whole house. After all, what was there to plug in, except maybe a radio?

Night after night it would grow dark, but a perfectly good bulb and wiring made no difference. We continued carrying kerosene lamps from room to room.

Then it finally came. What excitement there was in going through the house to try each light. It was a miracle to pull a switch and have light.

Perhaps the Spirit coming into our lives is something like that.

One of my daily chores, as a small boy, was to start out in the late afternoon sun to find the Jersey cows in some eighty acres of black jack (scrub oak) timber and grassland. Walking or riding a horse through sandburs and buffalo grass and tumbleweeds, I sometimes came upon a cow that had a tiny calf with her. Those who raised me always told me that these cows simply "found" a calf. I can recall looking around the place where I had spotted the cow to see if I could find another calf. But to my puzzlement, an old Jersey cow could always surpass me in this ability to find a baby calf.

They told me this fiction, I am sure, because they thought it would corrupt the morals of a tiny boy to know the truth.

There was not too much I enjoyed about high school, but playing basketball was one thing that seemed to "perk it up." I loved to dribble and shoot and compete in that kind of contest. Although never fleet afoot nor springy in jump, I was tall and fairly accurate in pushing the ball up and through the net.

One fellow that played for our team was even taller than I, and skinnier. It did not take long in a game for him to grow tired. The coach had to take him out, or soon we were having to appeal to the referees for a "time out."

The problem that we often face, off the court, is the failure to call the "time out."

It is different now. I fail to see the nobility of war. I fail to see how anyone seriously seeking to walk in the Way can become a professional killer. Then I felt differently.

Those who raised me took pride in contributing to the war effort. In the midst of World War II, they considered anything less than total commitment to the war cowardly, and those who by conscience objected they looked on as unfit to live in the community. We saved grease, gathered scrap rubber and scrap metal. While we would have raised cattle and hogs to make a living, it meant much more to see it as our contribution to the war effort. Along with others we sang "Praise the Lord and Pass the Ammunition." My family was scrupulously honest during the period of food rationing. With the amount of food grown on the farm, this was no particular problem except for a teen-ager who liked sugar. To solve the problem of running out of sugar each month, when they had set aside enough for cooking and canning, they then distributed the rest in pint jars, given to each of us. Right in front of our plates each meal was a pint jar with sugar that had to last a month! It always disturbed me to find mine the first one empty. That war still affects me in that I have been bothered when I have seen my children heaping teaspoons of sugar extravagantly on their cereal or into their iced tea. They could have indulged in other excesses, and it would not have so pained me.

The Vietnam War may have been longer and may have unleashed more bombs. It may have entered our living rooms by way of television, but it never had the sense of cause and of waging war against a totally evil enemy that characterized the Great War.

Besides, through America's longest war, I enjoyed all the sugar I wanted.

It was my first encounter with New York City. Eager was I to see all the big-city sights that had become familiar landmarks—Wall Street, the Bowery, China Town, and so on. At my hotel, I looked over the brochures of various tour agencies. Finally, I spotted one that pictured the Statue of Liberty along with other desirable sights. It was rather expensive, but it was advertised as a glass-domed observation bus, and I thought it would be worth it.

When I boarded it, I found the glass-domed, ultramodern bus was really an old converted school bus with a canvas top. After seeing several interesting places, we were driven to what was of primary significance to me, the Statue of Liberty. But we stopped at the edge of Manhattan, and the guide pointed out through a dense, moist fog to where the statue could be seen on a clear day. Straining, we could see just a shadowy glimpse of something. It was probably there, but I could not verify it.

While in the brochure it was pictured clearly, in full color, in the reality we experienced, it was about as inexplicit as the religious life of most people.

Driving through the most elegant and exclusive part of a city one day, where the lawns were immaculately coiffured and greens placed with an artist's touch, I observed to my companion, "These are certainly some of the best homes I have ever seen."

My companion was quick to correct me: "Some of the best houses."

Stunning simplicity. The youth had introduced the speaker for the evening, giving his name and saying only, "Now, we'll see what he can do." And more to the point than a table of schools attended.

The chaplain at the federal reformatory in El Reno, Oklahoma, was telling me about the strange situation he encountered in that institution. Pages were missing from the New Testaments that had been distributed in Cell House B. They had been carefully removed. That cell contained the disciplinary problems. Stripped of privileges, the young offenders were permitted only the Bible as reading material.

Surely, one would not be surprised that prisoners would select certain passages to hold close and memorize, but that was not quite the explanation. Somehow the youths acquired bits of tobacco, then used the pages as cigarette papers. On fire with the Word.

There is this report about Beau Brummell, the famous British dandy of the eighteenth century: "It took him four hours to get dressed, and he dressed three times a day." An age of Jockey shorts and Levis and undressing has difficulty comprehending what Beau Brummell was doing.

The man's sermon was a travesty on the Christian faith. Afterward, a kindred soul was effusive in praise. The preacher replied, "Don't give me the credit. It was all the Holy Spirit."

I hope not. I honestly doubt the Holy Spirit was flattered with such credit.

What we read of the Church of the Saviour in Washington, D.C., draws us to quote and praise but not to imitate.

Waves of satisfaction swept over me as I read a news report of an attorney suing the photographer at his wedding because the pictures of his bride were so "grotesque and repulsive" that they caused trouble with his in-laws and loss of money in his private practice.

Having witnessed a few weddings, having been a groom in a wedding, and having officiated at a few weddings, I have come to realize that weddings are staged primarily for photographers. Perhaps it was not always so, but they have infiltrated every nook of the ceremony. They present evidence themselves of being in the bride's dressing room while she is getting her garter girt. They leave exposed the emotional condition of the waiting groom's company. And in the midst of the ceremony's sacredness, pop! there is a clatter and a light explosion. Then, after the couple have been declared husband and wife, members of the wedding party march back to the altar to respond mechanically to each direction—move there, stand here, smile, a little to the left, look at her eyes . . .

This aggression should be stopped. As Dean Rusk always warned about these things, if we do not stop it now, our children and our grandchildren will be living with photographers.

Halloween is just not the same these days although there is a discreet degree to which you share the direction of difference with your offspring. Well past my twentieth birthday was I before I heard the presentday beggar's chant "trick or treat!" Now I find Halloweens pale, but comfortably so, in comparison to those of my younger days.

Excitement came with those Halloween nights! On reflecting though I sometimes wonder what made pushing over privies such great sport. The Freudian could probably give an entertaining analysis of privy tipping, but until that happens, one must be content with mere reminiscence. Some day, someone will probably trace that, also, back to Pope Gregory III in the eighth century.

When my daughter was small, I went with her and two other little girls on the Halloween circuit. I became their protector as they made the rounds of the neighborhood to "trick or treat." My position was usually out near the street, unseen by residents as they opened their doors to the girls. One of the girls had a coin box for UNICEF, and at the start, she was always careful to ask for a gift for UNICEF. Even then, she received her share of candy. Toward the end of the evening, the girl, still having the box in her hand, failed to ask for a contribution. The lady of that house generously contributed candy, and the girls turned to rush away. "What about UNICEF?" the lady asked.

"Oh, tha's O.K.," the girl called back, "I've got enough."

The lady reflected aloud, to no one in particular, "I wonder when you get enough." Her question still speaks to me.

It's hard to club a nun. That is why she is so effective in a demonstration.

When a pastor is caught as a thief, or runs off with a woman of the parish, the church press is remarkably silent. In that silence, the ecclesiastical press is quite unlike the secular press which feeds upon the human foible. It is even more unlike the Bible which records the sins of all—from an obscure Ananias to the heroic David.

This is not a plea for a church scandal sheet; it is simply an observation.

It is well to remember too that most of the church press is a "kept" press, that is, it is employed by the denomination. For this reason, it tends to hold denominational officials less accountable and less open to criticism than the public press does public officials.

The late Walter Winchell ran a daily newspaper column with rather loose and breezy copy. When a reporter from a rival newspaper charged untruths in the column and invited Winchell to reply, the famous one said, "I don't care about what small-timers think of me, I'm more interested in what the president thinks."

Gad! It's tough to be a small-timer.

"Tell it like it is," they say. Why not tell it like it could be? Be part of the "Now" generation, the "in" voice tantalizes. Why not enlarge life and be part of the "Not Now" generation?

When our oldest son was graduating from high school, we anticipated that moment of graduation. We looked forward to seeing him in cap and gown at baccalaureate and commencement, but the dreams of parents, as we discover, are not always the visions of the children. He did not choose to go to baccalaureate. He did finally decide to go to commencement but only, he assured us, because of our wishes.

Why the lack of interest in ritual celebration? I am not certain. It may be that we experienced more struggle and more suffering in his completing high school than he did and thus were more ready to enter into celebration. Surely, celebration comes as a result of our being intensely involved and at a level that brings suffering. Of course, it may be that he too would have celebrated, but the rituals which were prescribed for him did not offer the opportunity for celebration.

When going to a new job, there has frequently come to me the question, Are you getting adjusted to your new work? The proper answer to this query is simply yes, but there is something within that impels me to avoid that simple answer. With that question, I have a genuine problem. Having never been very well adjusted anywhere, I cannot imagine becoming well adjusted in any task I undertake.

It may be my own malady that makes me enjoy and feel the most comfortable in the presence of other persons who are unadjusted and insecure. Those persons so secure they appear to have complete command of themselves and the situation just have no cracked or chipped-away point in their structures where I can take a toehold.

How surprised Cyrus would have been to be told by Isaiah that his conquests were for the benefit of Hebrew prisoners. That would be like telling Stalin that the death toll at Stalingrad was not on behalf of Russians but on behalf of Jewish inmates of Auschwitz. It would be like telling Roosevelt that the campaign against Japan was only that a few Chinese prisoners might be released.

When I read *Crime and Punishment*, I wonder, why will a girl like Sonia love a murderer like that Raskolnikoff? Why will she follow him even to prison? There is no knowing. But there is miracle, as if he were resurrected from the dead, for Raskolnikoff discovers love within himself.

It always makes me feel good to see headlines about a minister being involved in extortion or bribery or theft or something of the sort. It means that people at least do not expect our profession to be so involved. Now, if it were a banker or a lawyer or an insurance man, we would probably expect it, and it would not make headlines—just a little column near the want ads.

Some years ago, when I was a member of the Junior Chamber of Commerce in Fredonia, Kansas, I joined with others in a national project of the Jaycees, "Putting Christ Back into Christmas." Our local club worked at that, although it escapes me what we did. As I think about it, it seems ironic for a businessman's organization to wage a campaign against the commercialization of Christmas. I am not aware of any long-term results of that project.

The fullness of joy comes when we feel we have created. How much greater is that joy than when we know we have been merely good.

To be in the crisp air and view the snow on the mountains; to discover what is genuinely funny and laugh until your sides hurt and your eyes make tears; to smell another person or plant; to know for a brief time the genuine gnawing of hunger; to find an abandon and a release in sexual passion and expression; to hold a baby next to your face; to be aware of the water pelting your skin while taking a shower; to vibrate with the beating of a drum or the notes of an organ; to grieve genuinely at the death of a loved one; to walk into the breeze and let your hair be blown; to ache with stretched muscles that are not often used; to enjoy the touch or the embrace of another person; to be out of breath from strenuous running or climbing—how rich is the gift of God in these sensuous, emotional, and physical experiences. Unlike Buddhism, the aim of the Christian faith is not to transcend human feeling and experience. The senses are not to be escaped; they are for our fullness.

Most of what I know, I cannot remember.

The above truth accounts for my preservation and reference to a statement that appeared in *Nation's Business*, June 1964:

> Don't envy the man in your company who has a prodigious memory. Chances are he is a poor creative thinker. An expert on memory, Dr. James Birren says research indicates that there is a correlation between the mind crammed full of details about the past, and the lack of here-and-now creativity. "To keep your mind up-to-date, you have to have some decays of your older memories," he said. "In other words, to be flexible and creative, the mind needs new inputs of knowledge to discipline old ones."

This statement does not improve my plight, but it tickles my fantasy about it.

Events

Golgotha was the scene of history's most noted case of capital punishment.

A vote for the Lord.

In 1968, I attended a district conference of churches in the Southeast. A major agenda item was merger with a neighboring district. The district board was recommending it, and the other district involved had already given approval.

The issue was heatedly debated. As an outsider, the issue was of no great moment to me. For me, it was not a matter of asking if I wanted to enlarge my family. For me, it was not a matter of having to deal with treasured memories. Those kinds of considerations made it *very* important, crucial, to those deliberating. My own interest was caught in the way the decision was being made.

When the exchange of debate and discussion seemed

complete, there was some conferring at the front of the room. Then the presiding officer announced: "We'll now take the vote. All those who favor merger and having unity in the church and progress in the future and the will of God, please stand." Twenty-three persons stood. After counting, the presider called for the negative vote, saying, "Those opposed to the merger, stand." Nine stood.

That's what is called "putting the question"!

As I made notes of the very words used in putting the question, I reflected upon it as illustrative of a common tendency among us. Spoken or unspoken, we see our conviction on an immediate issue as carrying enormous weight. A certain openness to the Spirit might suggest that the nine opposed voted, thinking they also were favoring unity and progress and the will of God. Or, what is more sobering yet, our decision may have very little to do with these idealized goals.

Some seven or eight miles from our farmhouse in Oklahoma was a grange hall. It was a little wooden structure atop a small sand hill and surrounded by black jack timber. I must have been eight or nine years old when a revival was held there. An evangelist came and people called him "high-powered." And he was not alone. With him was a large Negro woman; people called her a fat nigger woman. She led the singing, but that was not all! Folks said both she and the evangelist, once the fiery sermon reached its end, talked in tongues, and shouted, and rolled in the aisles. And somehow, others did the same, once it started.

This sounded like quite a show, and I was glad when I was included with several grown-ups going to the revival meetin'.

Sing! They could sing and make those thin walls quiver as that giant black woman led "Bringing in the Sheaves" and "When the Roll Is Called Up Yonder." The sermon was loud and long, but at least the point was obvious to me: I was headed for hell.

But from that point on, it was a disappointment. There was no speaking in tongues, no rolling or jumping—only shouting. We felt cheated as we left, failing to see and hear that which we had expected.

In some early civil rights work, I joined in the effort of the Human Relations Department of Kansas City. The aim was to secure integrated services in restaurants.

One assignment had us carrying questionnaires to every snack shop and café in the city, asking if they would serve regardless of race. For those who said yes, there was a further test. Two of us, a black and a white, would have lunch or dinner there.

In just such a test, a promising, brilliant young black and I went to a café, were seated, and after a time were served. Later, in evaluating the event as we were instructed to do, my companion thought he detected some hesitancy in our being served. I had not noticed, for it seems to be the way of restaurants that they keep you waiting long enough to build your appetite beyond what you had planned to eat when you entered earlier in the day.

But there is the dilemma: The black does not know. Was the delay because of his race or because things are just that way?

My neighbor may avoid me or curse me, and there may be a reason. The same may be true of the black. But even if the factors are the same, the black in this society never knows. He is apt to chalk it up to his being black. All children fight, but if in a mixed group the black child is hit, his parents are apt to think it is because he is black.

This is one way that the black becomes racist, that is, interprets life as racially determined. True, he has suffered most from the exploitation of race. Now that improvement has come, the black still is not free. He is still exploited, and he has added to him an additional burden—he is in a position to do some of the exploiting.

March 1, 1954, on one of the Marshall Islands in the Pacific, there was a thermonuclear explosion equal to twelve and one-half million tons of TNT. The explosion was six hundred times greater than the atomic bomb which devastated Hiroshima.

A Japanese fisherman, seventy-one miles away from the island, reported that as he and seven of his mates were pulling in the nets they suddenly saw great sparks and fire as bright as the sun itself. The sky around them glowed fiery red and yellow. After several minutes, the yellow seemed to fade away, and there was left a dull red, like a piece of iron cooling in the air. Then there was a giant blast which sounded like many thunders rolled into one. A pyramid cloud began to rise, and soon the sky was clouded over.

The men went back to their fishing.

Two hours later a fine ash began to descend upon them. By the time they reached port in Japan, they were feeling the effects of radiation. The most severely injured men were showing a sharp decline in their white corpuscle count.

A report such as this needs a title. Could it be "National Security" or "Peace With Honor" or "Making the World Safe for Democracy"?

1958. St. Stephen's Baptist Church, Kansas City. The speaker was Thurgood Marshall. Purpose: raising funds for the National Association for the Advancement of Colored People.

Following Marshall's measured but eloquent speech, a local black minister appealed for funds. He told of being in a shoe store a few days before and of discussing some of the atrocities being visited upon their people. After one particularly brutal episode was mentioned, the shopkeeper said, "That just makes my blood boil!"

The minister said that he had come to the conclusion that "too many Negroes have boiling blood without doing anything about it." Then he turned to the some three thousand people in the congregation, nearly all black, and said, "When you see Governor Faubus keeping little girls out of school with bayonets, does that make your blood boil?"

As with one voice and purpose, the congregation answered, "Yes, yes." There were no passive listeners. They were in it. They were participating. They encouraged the speaker by urging him on.

And he did go on. He mentioned a couple more racial problems, leaving the audience with the question, "Does that make your blood boil?" Each time, they responded with a quicker tempo and louder voice, "Yes, yes."

"Does it make your blood boil when you see Governor Almond haul down the American flag and run up the flag of Virginia over that commonwealth's capitol building?"

"Yes, yes," they say.

"When they will kill a man who stole less than two dollars, does that make your blood boil?" (He referred to a murder of a black man by whites.)

Louder than ever they shout, "Yes! Yes!"

Then with a triumphant smile, baring white teeth that fairly gleamed, the minister quietly said, "Then get out your money."

That man knew how to call for the offering. It is something most of us have never learned.

On two occasions in the early 1960s, a black congregation in Kansas City invited me to preach. There is a significance in receiving a second invitation. Never forget that. Almost anyone can get the first. Prior to these invitations, I had been in the pew but never the pulpit of a black church.

As I began to speak, it was startling to hear people shouting back to me. It took me a piece of time to adjust to the ricocheting returns of "Amen!" "Praise the Lord!" and such. As I moved toward transition, I found the restraints were loosening. I was becoming free. I was being given wings to sail. They pulled from me more than I had known before.

Looking back, I have realized that they were not blanketing with endorsement all that was being said. It was not that academic. Rather, they were expressing their own deep will that the preacher proclaim God's Word, and they were participating in the proclamation.

During the last week of May 1973, a madman's hammer struck the marble in St. Peter's Basilica in Rome. Crying, "I am Jesus Christ," Lazlo Toth set about to destroy Michelangelo's Pietà. In a matter of moments, a man marred the beauty that inspired people for four hundred years. He marred the finest creation of the world's most creative sculptor.

Why is it that men do their Inquisition with His name on their lips?

On January 15, 1966, Nigeria, the model of Western democracy for Africa, shocked the world by having its first military coup. I landed in Lagos, capital of Nigeria, that day, a day I shall never forget. The next day was Sunday. Attending church and then walking the streets, I encountered a young Nigerian just leaving church, carrying his hymnbook.

He greeted me pleasantly, asking if I were British.

"No," I said, "American."

His expression changed. And in the conversation that followed, he bombarded me with charges and questions. "When are you going to quit killing my people in America?" "When are you going to quit discriminating against my people?" "When are you going to let them buy a house where they want to?" "Why do you turn dogs on my people?"

I tried to explain that I shared his concern, that it was not I who was doing these things that were then so much in the news. He would have none of it. He heard my words only as excuses. He said, "You speak of you, individually. I speak of you corporately."

One of the lessons of travel is that you cannot go alone; you take your nationality with you. I became aware that day in Nigeria, as never before, of my corporateness.

If you ever want to relive a battle of the Civil War, go to Gettysburg, Pennsylvania. Surely there are more ways to see the carnage of battle at Gettysburg than at any other battlefield in the world. Exhibits slice the event every way: they examine every general down to his little toenail; they mark every cannon and how many bolts held it together; they analyze the weather, the uniforms, the food, the flesh of the men down to the moles and birthmarks. They put you in the middle of the bluecoats and the graycoats until you can see and smell and feel the battle.

In a main pavilion of the battleground, there is a panorama of all this death and an unseen voice narrating. It concludes that men from both North and South won honor and glory for their nation at Gettysburg.

Honor? That is a puzzling statement. Three days' battle took its toll in the lives of fifty-three thousand men. As death comes to man after man, where is the honor? Where is the glory? What did it all achieve? Did that blood mean anything?

The blood of One, shed for his enemies not against them, meant reconciliation with God, according to the tentmaker.

God has done an amazing thing! He has loved us while we were yet sinners, while we are yet sinners. That's an amazing, surprising event.

The world is not like that. Not the world we know. The world we know is one of charge and countercharge. The world we know is one of hatred and counterhatred, of being ignored and ignoring. The world we know is one of constant evaluation for performance—on the job, on the highway, at home, as a lover. And if our performance does not measure up, there is no acceptance.

⚬❪Trends❫⚬

For as long as memory serves me, the rage in sermons, articles, and books has centered around *change.* Change is observed, predicted, affirmed, chanted. The breadth and intensity of the discourse suggest a compelling fascination and fixation that would mark the attention of a groom for his bride of one hour.

Recognizing the vicissitudes of theological thought and the tradition wherein the true prophet stands over against the popular prophets, it seems to me that to be ahead of the game and truly prophetic, one needs to herald and develop a no-change stance.

The basic thesis could be stated in trinitarian form. There has never been any change. There is no change. There will never be any change.

The next step, as any preacher knows, is to find a text to support the thesis. (We could begin with a text and see where it leads us, but that would be confusing and might end where we do not intend.) Just opening the Bible at random, we find in the first chapter of Ecclesiastes:

A generation goes, and a generation comes,
  but the earth remains for ever.
The sun rises and the sun goes down,
  and hastens to the place where it rises. . . .
What has been is what will be,
  and what has been done is what will be done;
  and there is nothing new under the sun.
Is there a thing of which it is said,
  "See, this is new"?
It has been already in the ages before us.

It would also be helpful to find scriptural support in the New Testament. This proves to be no insurmountable problem. There is the passage from Hebrews: "Jesus Christ is the same yesterday and today and for ever" (Heb. 13:8). And what of the critical conditions of life? Again we are covered. "You always have the poor with you" (Matt. 26:11) and "you will hear of wars and rumors of wars" (Matt. 24:6). Nothing has changed. Nothing will change.

A favorite pattern in illustrating change is to reflect on how different things are than they were in the speaker's childhood. This is precisely the most convincing part of the no-change position. Let me illustrate how things have not changed. The unrest of students on major university campuses has been directed in large measure toward the system of huge, impersonal classes; they make things more intimate with sit-ins. At the university level, as at other educational levels, much attention is being given to the small class-size and individual attention. The direction is exactly the same as my personal experience. During most of my eight years at Round Grove grade school, there were only two of us in the class, and we often had more personal attention than we wanted.

Even the school facilities have not changed. For example, the new school buildings have central heating. Round Grove also had central heating, and on cold days, we gathered around the heating unit while the teacher kept it at capacity with thermostatic wood chunk after thermostatic wood chunk. Things are static. They have not changed; they will not change.

Finally, it is necessary to make a few predictions for the future and to suggest the way the church can be relevant (holy term) in the future.

What will life be like in coming decades? The same as it is now. Those who can remember 1929 and the early 1930s will be expecting the Great Depression to return. The *Chicago Tribune* will be fighting government spending and communism and taking a few editorial cracks at the Daughters of the American Revolution for being too liberal. Zsa Zsa Gabor will look a beautiful thirty years old as she takes a new husband, another new husband, and another new husband. People will be saying that someone ought to be doing something about our natural resources, air, water, land, and vegetation. Others will be concerned about the rising crime rate, insisting that personal armories have nothing to do with killings but that fault lies with laxity in the courts. Wars will be caused by the aggression of foreigners.

As for relevance in the church, the secret is to avoid changing a thing. The temptation will be to take the easy route of just doing things differently than we did in the past. The word of hope is no-change.

A pastor reported to the General Offices of the Church of the Brethren in 1964 that he could report in his church an increase in attendance from the previous quarter of *one-tenth of 1 per cent.* And this, he said, definitely proves the trend is up! Some cynics would look at that and pass it off, "Figures lie and liars figure." Or someone else will protest that you cannot measure the mission of the church in percentages.

That fellow has something. With an average attendance zooming along at 41.2 per Sunday compared with only 41.1 last quarter, he has caught a trend in an embryonic stage. And more important, he has a trend within manageable grasp. In other words, to establish such a trend, the pastor himself probably brought his mother-in-law to the morning worship service in the second quarter. Or maybe the population exploded in the parsonage and the minister's wife brought the new baby one Sunday.

If one-tenth of 1 percent gives us a trend, we can at least help determine something.

The city of Elgin, Illinois, lies along the Fox River. Built beside that river, at the south edge of the business district so that the city's main street marched directly toward it, was a bastion of a building known as the Elgin Watch Factory. High on the front of the structure was the face of a clock that gave the time to that community for decades. Elgin had been known and respected around the world. When international guests came to the city, typically they wanted to see the Elgin Watch Company.

Today, as the Fox River passes the place where the old brick structure stood, there is a sadness. The clock no longer strikes, its parts have gone to a museum in Denver. The walls of the building one day "came tumblin' down." Some day from amid the rubble and weeds may arise a new form of building—if buildings know a resurrection from the dead.

Perhaps it is a sign to us who live and die by the clock and the calendar. There is another kind of time not so directly tied to the fortunes of business and its vacillating needs.

Something is happening in the church today—a movement toward a church that is tougher and leaner. The fat that had accumulated in fashionable days and gave us a stance of being jolly is dropping away. The new diet tastes narrow and judgmental to some, but to others it is a chance for life, prescribed by the Great Physician. The uncritical, all-embracing, world-affirming style that took its cue from what "feels good" felt comfortable but left us vulnerable to a heart attack. That style is in the process of passing as the muscles of the church are flexed and punished, as we no longer lounge comfortably as before a television set, taking in beer and football. Now we must run.

A friend of mine has said something that has been of immense help to me. Occasionally he has said, "I've changed my mind on that." How easy it is to become locked into a position because we have said something on an issue and feel the need to continue to defend what was said even when we gain a new and different insight. While one needs some stability of thought, it offers a new freedom to realize that it is not required that we stay with the same mind always.

Seminaries have been in a critical condition for as long as I can remember. There is a report, probably not true, that when John the Baptist entered the Zion Seminary, it was thought to be the last class because of accelerated costs and because so few young men were planning to enter the ministry.

The crisis is not new. The program is. I understand they have developed a whole new curriculum. The required subjects are these:

Basic Beliefs in Nonviolent Ways to Provoke Violence
Greek and Hebrew Profanity
The Cocktail Hour
Picket-line Administration
Feeling the Sensitive Places
Denominational Demolition (a major in this course features thirty-seven perspectives on the irrelevance of the denomination and leads to the D.D. degree)

Of course, there is an elective—the Bible. The instruction is practical. Ministers have to be taught how to avoid being the chore-boy and running errands so they can assume the servant role. Once we studied the God of

Abraham, Isaac, and Jacob; now it's *Lord of the Flies*. Once we quoted St. Paul and St. Francis; now it's St. Holden Caulfield, St. Fanny Hill, and St. Peter Drucker.

A few people are concerned about what is happening but without reason. This is probably the last class.

Do the footprints of faith pattern in a straight line? Probably not. There is a going back and forth, a sensitivity that is prone to movement. There is a greater value in being obedient than in being fully consistent. There is awareness that those fully consistent become wedded to this age but widowed to the next age. The footprints of faith may be here today and there tomorrow. We are called to declare, "Here I stand." In retrospect, it may also be necessary to say, "There I stood."

°❦[Images]❦°

My memory is still vivid of an early experience in art.
I was in the second or third grade in a little one-room
country school out on Oklahoma's plains. There were
about thirty of us scattered across eight grades and well-
carved benches and desks.

One day the teacher passed out sheets on which were
outlined a Dutch boy and tulips. We were all to color this
same drawing, and the best ones in each grade were to be
posted on the wall. This was a challenge, and I devoted
myself to those crayons to make the most beautiful picture
of all. I don't think I was overly confident, but if the
teacher were going to post several of them, I was sure
mine would be among them, and it might even be the best.

We handed in our creations and had to wait until the
next morning for results. I remember coming into the room
and seeing Dutch boys and tulips all over the wall, but I
looked and looked and never found mine. I could not
understand it. Something must have happened. So finally,

sometime during the day, I asked the teacher why mine was not on the wall.

She told me. She brought out my paper and pointed out that I colored outside the lines. Sure enough, I had. Funny, I never even realized it until she told me. Not only that, I colored one arm of the boy's shirt with one color, and the other arm, still another color. Yes, I did that.

Now my wife has tried to reassure me about that experience, saying that today people would probably call that kind of coloring creative. As for the shirt sleeves, they might even be accurate for the new styles.

But it may be that one has to learn that the lines are there before there is really freedom to be creative outside them.

I am reminded of the way they used to break horses to ride. They would let them run wild until they were two or three years old, then turn them over to someone whose job it was to "break" them.

Men who could break a horse were heroes to us boys. They all seemed to be tall, lean, and muscular. With a special bit for the horse's mouth and with big swells on his saddle against which he braced his legs, such a man could ride a fairly wild horse, but it was a dangerous business, and they were not always successful. There were some horses that could never be tamed, could never be trusted to an ordinary rider.

Now there is a gentler way. A halter is put on the horse when he is just a young colt. Things are placed on his back, like a sack of hay, then a saddle blanket, then the

saddle. Slowly the process builds until the young horse·
reaches such maturity that a man can climb into the saddle,
and the horse is ready for it.

It would be tempting to draw a parallel with the conversion experience. That temptation must be resisted.

Some see the faith as milquetoast, something that can be
taken and will not upset the spiritual stomach. It is to calm
and soothe the ulcers that the world has placed there. They
see the faith as milquetoast rather than as a nut whose rich-
est meat is not exposed, whose enjoyment requires getting
beyond the outer shell, whose nourishment awaits one who
would run well the race of life.

Some see the faith as a marshmallow. It is soft and com-
forting. It surrounds every blow and never stands steady
for any bite. It is sweet and nice and white. They see the
faith as a marshmallow rather than meat that is sometimes
tender, sometimes tough, but always with its measure of
protein. It also carries with it that which is less suited to
our taste—the bone and the gristle.

Some see the faith as a Currier and Ives print where
nothing is disturbed. The landscape is beautifully covered
with snow: the smoke and grime of the factory have not
darkened it; the blood of dead soldiers has not reddened
it; the ache of old age has not yellowed it. It is a placid
Eden with a little white church and man and beast, all
without distracting motion. There is no serpent on the
horizon. They see the faith as Currier and Ives rather than
the photography of Ed Wallowitch. The lens of that man
captures the lines of loneliness of an old woman seated on

a park bench. It shows us a young boy in the city slums, his head lifted and carrying a lily. There is a radiance on the boy's face. The slum is still there, but the feeling and the power of the resurrection has broken through the walls of poverty, and the triumph comes to focus in a lily and a lad's face. Wallowitch uses the shadows *of life to expose what is triumphant.*

Some see the faith as the mellow tones of Everett McKinley Dirksen, his vocal chords massaged with vaseline, waxing poetical and eloquent on the virtues of the marigold. Some see the faith in mellow tones rather than in the sharp voice of a William Sloane Coffin warning that many of our people are paralyzed and scared in their thinking.

Some see the faith as a tuxedo. It is straight, slick, and proper. It is unwrinkled. It dresses up the most outrageous of forms. It is a faith that is only temporary; it is rented and then taken back or put away until another dress-up occasion. It never really feels like it belongs to us; yet it is impressive to the ladies and the cameras. Some see the faith as a tuxedo rather than Levis designed for living and working. There is no fear of their getting dirty; with them you can change a tire or dig in the yard—and the dirt, the stain that clings there while the living is being done—well, Levis can be washed, and it really doesn't matter much if they are a little dirty if in the process the task is completed. And one can enjoy the feel of the toughness of the fabric.

Some see the faith as a Strauss waltz. It has beautiful balance. The notes are rounded and easy flowing. They bring to mind grand old Vienna, plush and ornate. How beautiful are the women in their long gowns as they glide across the floor. Some see the faith as a Strauss waltz rather than the theme music from *Dr. Zhivago*. The latter begins with the dark tramping of laboring feet. It includes the tender and affectionate feeling for Lara. And there is something in the body of the music that speaks of endurance. Or there is *Porgy and Bess* with its genuine tragedy, its distress without being overcome.

The world is richer for the Strauss waltz, Currier and Ives, and marshmallows. Even Everett McKinley Dirksen. We are right to enjoy them. Indeed they can be a source of comfort. But they are poor reflections of life's reality or of a faith to cope with that reality. A Savior who was beaten by soldiers, ridiculed, and lynched calls forth a faith that has the wearing and toughness of denim, the truth of a prophet, and a perspective that sees the light because it is also aware of the shadow and the darkness.

Western movies have ridden beyond the Great Divide. For the most part, they are no longer innocent; they have lost the simplicity of easy good and sinister evil.

The Marshal Dillon of "Gunsmoke," the Gary Cooper of *High Noon*, the Alan Ladd of *Shane*, all represent or epitomize the classic Western. That's true although "Gunsmoke" and *Shane* began to cheat a little on the formula: Dillon frequents the bar and the barmaid; Shane's romance is with another man's wife, a love from which he must ride away into the sun.

The hero of the old Western was broad-shouldered, clean-shaven, well groomed, wearing light-colored clothes. His hat looked like the silver-belly Open Road Stetson. No one needed to tell you that he was the hero, the good person. You knew it immediately. A three-year-old knew.

Then came the villain. He slumped in the saddle. Boisterous. He banged through the saloon doors. There were no women to love him. His clothes were dark—including the hat. No one needed to tell you, "This is the evil one." You knew it. A three-year-old knew it.

How much has the Western formula entered our mindset? Surely something akin to it colors our self-image, personally and nationally. The gospel is less simple. It suggests that it is not so easy to divide and separate the good guys from the bad. Oh, there are images of final judgment that suggest such division, but with that there is no easy human recognition; rather, there is human surprise. Paul puts it rather starkly to the Romans, "All have sinned and fall short of the glory of God" (Rom. 3:23).

Not that there are no differences in men. There are.

One would hope the new Westerns will give us more depth in character, will show us ambiguity in morality, mixed motivation, and something more realistic than physical appearance in identifying good and evil.

A parish newsletter crossed my desk. It carried a lament from the pastor. (Thank God for that personal word; communications from the church too often resemble a clipping service of *Christian Herald* poetry and half-clever negatives like "The World's Beatitudes" copied from a Vermont church's newsletter who had picked it up from a church in Georgia, who . . .) He had attended a meeting of the denomination's district board of administration. It was, he said, mostly concerned with finances. When, he asked, would the board turn to spiritual matters?

I know the yearning. Why in the church do we not just feast at the Lord's Supper? Is there not some way that the Lord himself could arrange the meal, saying simply he has need of it, and it would appear? "This is my body which is given for you. Do this in remembrance of me" (see Luke 22:19). But how can bread become his body when money must be given the baker for it or when a crusty deaconess must stand over a stove to bake it?

Why in the church do we not rap only on the rapture, gaze only upon the transfigured Christ, and paint with oriental detail the joys of heaven? Even when we do it, some brute comes along and declares that it is twelve o'clock, or that the devil is loose again. Why, in my personal life, when I want to be serene and mystical and a holy man—why does God send me a sex drive and hunger?

Indeed, when will we turn to spiritual matters?

Fiddler on the Roof reflects on tradition. While it comes from a Jewish setting, it is of profit to those of us who identify with the Christian faith.

There is an inherent relation between tradition and the Christian mission. The stones, the reminders of tradition, are on this side of the Jordan. They call us, not back to Egypt, but to all the people of the earth that the Lord may be feared forever.

Tradition is our foundation. It is the bond between the present and the past, but more important, energy for the future. It is the fellowship that a person has with those of the faith in another time, another place, or the same time and place. It is our corporate memory. It is knowledge of what God has done.

They tell us that our word *idiot* comes from a Greek term meaning private, peculiar, alone. Only an idiot tries to understand the Christian faith outside the tradition which has accrued.

Sure. Tradition can become a tyrant. That is the nature of power. Better it is to try to harness that power than to go powerless.

The life of the party. We feel a compulsion to exude happiness and to give gaiety. If an image of us is to be retained, that is how we want it. Why does the photographer always remind us to smile, say *cheese* or *whiskey*, or some other term to fake the face into an expression of gaiety?

It is a mood that we desperately need; perhaps we choose to be pictured that way precisely because of our desperation. But there are deeper and more enduring moods and gifts: the sharing of reflective thought, the tears of suffering.

The vogue in dress styles, particularly in the fashion of women for they have been the most responsive to the new, finds a parallel in the faith of people. The vogue is the "in" fad, the very latest thing, the temporarily popular, by definition, not a dominant style, not one of universal usage.

Vogue in style carries the appeal and prestige of the snob, but it has not borne the test of time. In establishing trends, the vogue will influence the direction of all styles but will always tend to be more extreme than that which lasts.

Look at the current styles in vogue and to the counterpart in style. There is the *maxi* style in which we try to cover everything. It is doubtful whether this style can remain vogue very long because it has difficulty maintaining interest, just like speeches or books that try to cover everything become the dullest. The maxi stance in religion takes on every new idea or practice that comes along without ever having related it or incorporated it into our basic heritage. Therefore, it covers itself with all sorts of religious practice, with patriotism and the flag, with astrology, with pop psychology—anything that comes along in the world.

There is the *topless* mode that found its way not only into the nightclubs but also onto the beaches. Someone observed about this vogue in style that the breast must be more dangerous than the gun because there are far more attorneys and politicians working to cover the breasts than there are to control firearms. The topless stance in religion is to have lost the sense of transcendence. It is to deify the human. It is to lose touch with that power that is beyond us.

There is the *bottomless* style—again, largely from the entertainment field. The organs of reproduction are completely uncovered and unprotected. So far as our faith is concerned, we become bottomless when we take away the roots, the foundation, the heritage that is ours. And when we celebrate such a faith, it is likely to resemble entertainment, and for the church, it covers us very little so far as reproduction is concerned. It does not bring new life or lives into our fellowship.

The *nude look* is also vogue with us. It seems to be a growing fad. It has gone big with the motion picture industry. In some cases, they have cleverly presented nudity with so-called message films, and regardless of how pornographic it becomes, there are always those who can find some great, profound gem of truth placed just to the left of a naked navel. Not just on the screen. There are also now a number of nude communities. The nude stance in religion is openness. It is brought with an ideology that contends that being faithful is to be completely open and honest in the sense that you tell everyone exactly what you think of them or of some issue. The nude look does not stop with skin; it even peels back the skin and talks about guts—putting your guts right out on the table. But man was created in the image of God, and a part of that image is mystery. For each person there is to be that which is private and which forever remains mysterious to his fellows. To strip away all that mystery is to strip away a part of what it means to be a person.

The vogue passes quickly. Nehru jackets are a good example. The less extreme in dress, the conservative, if you will, is more likely to last and wear. In faith, it is the basic rather than the novelty that lasts.

Chess is among the most fascinating and complex games. They say it came from India around the seventh century.

Consistent with the mystery of the East, the pieces speak a language of their own.

Take the pieces, the king and the queen. Do they bear to us an idea about men and women? From an era long before women's liberation went public, we have a game in which the queen, the woman, is the power figure. She can move with the greatest freedom; she is the most feared. The king is something of a stodgy dolt. He can only move a space at a time, and all other pieces are forever having to protect him. Is there an anticipation of our new understanding of women?

And what of the bishop? Why does a bishop never move directly? He never confronts head-on. He always moves at an angle, and though he has considerable power, he often exercises that power when the opponent forgets he is there. What is it about bishops that gives them that style of play?

Or, the knights. They are strong, but they are erratic, moving first this way and then that. Must it be so with the beautiful people we make our heroes?

Even with royalty and church hierarchy on the board, there is to the game a democratic ideal. Thus, the lowly pawn, if it can make its way across the board, avoiding capture, and reach the final row, can take on any role it wants. It can even become a queen. So it was with Alice in Lewis Carroll's *Through the Looking-Glass*. She got to the eighth row and became Queen Alice. The pawn begins with a disadvantage, but with remarkable luck a few make it over into the promised land and a new nature.

That leaves only the castle, and to that we retire.

There is in the passage of light a resemblance to the way in which faith takes form in human experience.

Among some people, faith takes form as *opaque*. Being opaque means having a density or quality that does not permit light to pass through. It is a glass with a heavy black coating. We use the opaque to secure privacy and to protect us from heat and light.

To be *opaque* in faith means to draw the curtain. It is to cut off the sound of testimony. For Christians, it is to believe in Jesus Christ, but no one knows about it. It is to be embarrassed to talk with the neighbors about the man from Nazareth; it is to cleanse our speech of all religious jargon, lest we betray what we believe.

To be *opaque* in faith is to be solitary, alone. Opaque Christians think that everyone must do his own thing, that we are all so different we must each find our own way. Being opaque, no light passes through them, and they do not look for the light that might come from others. Opaque Christians are the "silent majority" who think there is injustice in the world, who think we need peace, but who do not act because they do not want to get religion mixed up in politics. They do not act because that is the responsibility of someone else. They leave it to the experts.

To be *opaque* in faith is to feel "arrived." It does not suggest movement or pilgrimage or discovery. There is no discovery because there are no clues, no peering in. It is like a well-defined statement, a creed. But it is not like a novel. In the midst of a novel, we resist those who would tell us its outcome. "Don't tell me!" we shout. We would discover for ourselves. But we do not discover from the opaque, and we do not search if we ourselves are opaque.

A game that our family has played through the years, especially when the children were younger, is "Guess What I'm Thinking Of." One person thinks of an object, and the others then ask questions to discover the object. For example, suppose you are thinking of a snail. Someone has a good clue when he or she asks, "Is it an animal?"

My family has sometimes accused me of thinking of weird objects or ideas or giving misleading clues. I am certain I would not do this, but if someone *were* to do it, it would be a game in opaque. It would be as if you held a faith in mind but to every question you answered no or you answered with a diversion. It would be as if Jesus, who came to reveal God, said, "I am thinking about what God is like," and to our every inquiry he responded with that which kept his knowledge secret.

We do not discover the divine in the opaque. We discover when we are asking questions, when we are seeking clues, and when there is some response from the other side, some passage of light.

Suppose in playing the game, "Guess What I'm Thinking Of," we answered the first question, "Is it an animal?" not simply with yes but with "Yes, it's an animal, and do you know what, I can reveal to you that it is a snail." The game then is destroyed by being *transparent*.

Some people have a *transparent* faith. Being transparent not only permits light to pass through, but it also permits full vision from this side to the other side. We put transparent glass in our windows to see the snow that tops the mountain a few miles away. We put our perishable groceries in transparent bags to be able to see them and their freshness or spoilage.

To be *transparent* in faith is to expose everything in a

flash and to see all in an instant. Transparent Christians believe in Jesus Christ and everybody knows it—the girl at the grocery check-out stand, the freeway driver, the person passing on the street. They talk incessantly about it. They have no sense of when another person may be ready to hear. Transparent Christians have their faith in a "baggie" and think they can deliver it unspoiled to anyone they meet. Transparent Christians make a fetish of openness, and they assume that if they could make perfectly clear every thought and every emotion they have experienced they would somehow fulfill the kingdom of God.

To be *transparent* in faith is to think that God can be known fully. There are those Christians who look upon Jesus of Nazareth as God, as all there was and is of God. Therefore, to look upon Jesus is really to see God fully. There are those Christians who look upon their knowledge of God as complete. For them the task of faith is simply to lay out that knowledge in front of those who have not yet seen the light.

To be transparent in faith has a quick appeal—like the tinsel that draws the eye to certain packages. The appeal is that faith can be fast and easy. But what can be seen quickly at a glance does not hold us. We do not feel the need to become involved. We do not participate in discovery. Faith remains surface, lacks depth, and does not acknowledge the extent to which God is beyond our grasp. Indeed, a transparent faith reflects neither the mystery in which men in their honesty have always encountered God nor the human brokenness which is inherent as we would reflect that divine image.

There is a quality better suited for our image of faith than either opaque or transparent. It is *translucent*. The translucent permits light to pass through, but it diffuses the light. It bends the light. It is like the windows of a church. The light passes through, but in its passing the light is changed so that it has a new character. The window does not create the light; yet it shapes and shades what we see of the light. We cannot see detail beyond the translucent; yet dimly we can see outlines, movement. It takes concentration to see, and it is only as we grant that concentration, following the shadows, exploring the forms, that we discover what is on the other side.

What does *translucent* mean when it comes to faith? To be *translucent* in faith is to experience an awe and fear of God. It is to identify with the Hebrew people who not only did not see God but prayed that God would not speak to them, lest they die. Translucent Christians believe in Jesus Christ and reflect him in what they say and do. They respect him enough that they do not seal him off in plastic, but he is there in shape and substance for those who are ready to discern and to discover.

Translucent Christians celebrate their own discoveries by permitting others to discover, knowing

> The poem hangs on the berry bush,
> When comes the poet's eye;
> The street begins to masquerade
> When Shakespeare passes by.
> —W. C. TANNETT
> "We See as We Are"

Translucent Christians are given to modesty because they recognize the bending of the light which they do; they know that it is never as bright as that blinding light along the Damascus Road that hits a person directly. Translucent

Christians, even while yearning for the true light that enlightens every man, have some appreciation for the prism of faith that reflects light in different colors. In fact, they realize that a single reflection can never be the totality.

So the secret Messiah comes to your house. The trumpets do not blare to announce his arrival, but he is made known to you in the breaking of bread. So the Rabbi tells a parable. You hear it again and understand anew. It unfolds and unfolds and unfolds and unfolds, always to expose some new grain, some new mark.

The images of the way light passes are of more than passing interest. In the passage of light we both receive and witness to our faith.